WHAT'S NEXT

A ROCKET SCIENTIST
GLIMPSES INTO THE BEYOND

Ralph Sherman Hagloch, B.Sc.,M.Sc.,P.Eng.

XZYZX Publishing Ltd.
Copyright 2018 by XZYZX Publishing Ltd
First Printed in 2018
Printed in the USA

Previous book by Ralph Hagloch:
"A Glimpse of the Dawn," Edmonton, Canada, 1992 (no longer in print)

The Publisher: XZYZX Publishing Ltd

Library and Archives Canada Cataloguing in Publication
Hagloch, Ralph Sherman, 1929 -, author
What's next: a rocket scientist glimpses into the beyond / Ralph Sherman Hagloch

Cover design Natasha Fordey
Author photo Jens Gaethje

Issued in print and electronic formats.
ISBN 978-1-7753028-0-3 (paperback) ISBN 978-1-7753028-1-0 (epub)

1.   Self-actualization (Psychology) 1. Biography

CONTENTS

INTRODUCTION

I have spent my life working at the cutting edge of engineering science, helping to send man to the moon, man up into the cosmos with the NASA Apollo Program; sending spacecrafts to explore the big outer planets of our solar system, and beyond. Equally, I have, in the last 50 years been journeying in the depths of what it means to be human. This book is about what that journey means, my experiences and revelations concerning Truth…

Many of my experiences, visions and dreams I began to understand only after I met John de Ruiter and began to realise how vital is openness of heart, softness of heart, kindness of understanding, to living in Truth; to grasping Reality. Before that my experiences were glimpses, invitations, mysteries and signs pointing to more. But how can I organise my many experiences, and all I've come to Know (so far) into something that makes some sense? That seems to be perplexing. If many of my experiences, realizations and musings seem disjointed or out of place time-wise, it's because I haven't gotten organised yet. (Maybe I never will get organized). How does one organize revelations which occurred widely spaced in time and became realized only much later? How does one describe a picture drawn in tiny fragments—a little here, a little there, over a 40-plus-year period—and finally assembled into something real? How do you take many experiences, some big, some small, some tiny, some mind-blowing, widely scattered in time and assemble them into a mosaic that forms a *really big picture?* It's like trying to assemble a giant picture puzzle when you don't have the final picture to look at. To me, chronology is not so important. Skipping around in time with my stories might be only the ramblings of an old guy. But glimpses of Reality, tiny realisations, mini-awakenings, although they may be widely scattered in time, are extremely important. They tie together, they add up to a picture of Reality, a mosaic of what is Real in the Profound. Glimpses are vital and precious to finding Reality. They add up to a *really big* picture. They are all invitations to more. Old guys skip around in their memories, or else they forget extensively, and we just say "Dementia". Or "Oops, I had a senior moment". Old guys have an arsenal of excuses which we can employ to explain away errant behaviour. Some people say "weird", some say "crazy", but we old guys proudly say "eccentric".

TIMES PAST

Here is a brief history of my life, my "story", as a person in this world (so far). I was born and raised on a homestead near Spirit River in northern Alberta, Canada. My mom was a beautiful hard working, hard driving pioneer woman. My sister had to take over running the household when she was eight because our mom was working in the fields. My sister soon learned how to keep all us brothers in line. I went through half of high school in Sexsmith, Alberta. My family owned the local dairy. We milked about 25 cows morning and night, separated the cream, bottled the milk and delivered it to the whole town seven days a week. I finished high school in Dover, Ohio, USA. After high school I spent six years in the US Air Force, earned a Bachelor of Science degree in Aeronautical Engineering in Indiana, and then spent a career in San Diego in the "Space Race". I was working with missiles and space launch experiments.

Somewhere, in the ups and downs of that industry, I studied pollution control management (pollution problems of air, water, solid waste, and noise), and worked a year as an Air Pollution Control Engineer for a county in California.

Then I went back to school and earned a Master of Science degree in Civil Engineering from the University of Utah. Later I moved back to Alberta, Canada, and spent another career in manufacturing oil and gas equipment. I'm still working part-time as an engineer since my official retirement: Mostly designing Highway Tanks for transporting dangerous goods. I tell people that missed "Freedom 55", and I missed "Freedom 65", but now I have a plan: I'm working on "Freedom 95." Or else I say, I am retired; my only hobby is working.

This is a brief history of my life experiences on a more profound level (phase 1, first thirty-some years). I was raised going to church. I tried to listen, but never could get very interested. I usually found that I was spending more of my focus on the structures holding up the roof (now I can design them) than on what the preacher was saying. When I was about 19 I walked away from church, and for the next 15-16 years I considered myself an atheist (or at least an agnostic). I got married, and we had three kids. When they became old enough for Sunday school, I started attending church again. (We both thought it would be good training for the kids.) After a time, a few things that the preacher was saying started touching my interest; so I began praying again. My basic prayer was, "God, if You're real I want to KNOW it. I don't want to go to this church week after week, wondering."

Then, in January 1966 ...

CHAPTER 1

AN AWAKENING

TIMES PAST

My eyes were suddenly opened in a very brief glimpse. This light burst upon me, and I instantly knew I was in the Presence of God. But It wasn't an individual. (I had always been taught that God was an individual entity.) It was different. It was MUCH different. The light was far brighter than any light I had seen or even imagined. It was as if my brightness indicators were charged up to the top; and still the light was beyond. It was brighter; *far brighter!* Looking back in my memory it seems that I still can't imagine how bright it was. And the light was different. It was a source, exceedingly bright at the center, the source gradually diminishing with distance away from the center, with no edge. How do you have a light *source* with no edge? Any light *source* you look at...a light bulb, a fire, an explosion, the sun...has an edge. Not this. It was like nothing I had ever seen nor even imagined. I was flooded with joy and gladness and love. Gladness at being in the Presence of God. Far more gladness than I had ever felt or even imagined. It was as if my gladness indicators were all charged up to the top, and still the charge went beyond. Way beyond! Gladness beyond gladness. Joy beyond joy.

At the same time, love was poured upon me. I loved back, a little. More love was poured on me, stronger. The next cycle was stronger. And the next. And the next. This rapidly became a whirlwind of love. Love beyond love. It became a tornado! It was too strong! Too much! My love-measuring devices---the sense of love, the feeling of love---were all broken. Blown! I was inundated, drowning! Too much! Turn it off! In all the years since then, I have, on a few occasions, experienced a similar flow of love in meeting or relating to another; but the intensity---while surprising, sometimes shocking---has been far, far less intense than what I experienced in that moment. But always a residue remains. (Many years later, after being with John de Ruiter for a while, I got to wondering: What would have happened to me if I had not stopped IT? Would I have been swallowed up in love? Would I have disappeared into....IT? Into the Light? By stopping the tornado of love, did I forfeit a truly awesome opportunity?)

At the same time, I could clearly see my responsibilities, here where I live, in the world. I had a family. I had a job that had to be worked. The mortgage had to be paid. All the household bills had to be taken care of. The lawn had to be mowed; the washer repaired. All the day-to-day duties needed to be done. They were all there, very clear. But I could see them down about 500 feet from where I was, with God; with the Light. This instantly put everything in perspective. None of my mundane responsibilities and duties were to be neglected. But their priorities, relative to being in the Presence, were all 'clearly' in second place. My responsibilities in living remained clear, firm. The responsibility of living in the Light did not negate them. But the responsibility of living in the Light does take first place. It is far more important!

I saw myself as a speck of Light; like a candle beside a sun. Or one of a hundred billion specks that constituted the Light. Looking back, remembering, the nearest thing I've seen in this physical realm is a picture of a cluster galaxy.

As quickly as this experience had come, it was gone. It was a very brief glimpse. But WOW! I KNEW something. Something awesome! Something astounding! I was asleep when it burst upon me. I was wide awake and jumping out of bed when it ended: I HAD to write something down! I wrote, **"We're afraid to believe, to REALLY believe! We're afraid it would be too wonderful!!"**

We're afraid to believe; afraid it would be too wonderful.

After these many years that glimpse remains clear, unalterable. Doubt was forever ended. The idea of doubt became a silly thought. When something is burned into your mind, your memory, your heart, it cannot be erased. It left a craving in my heart --- a monumental demand within me, a need to return to the Light. To BE in the Presence again. So I was left searching.

PRESENT TIME

I later realised that the veil was dropped momentarily and I was seeing a little glimpse of Reality.
Looking back through my "stories" I can see a thousand little decisions points where I could have turned more towards the Light or more towards my own "story". In most cases I had chosen my personal "story".

PHILOSOPHICAL COMMENT

Life, Truth, Reality is much greater, much vaster, than my old concept of God as an Entity, Supreme, remote and separate from me. I am a tiny part of IT. My reason, or opportunity, for being is to express that. To express what I've come to KNOW of the profound and of REALITY (so far). I think it was Mark Twain who said "the best two days of your life; the day you were born and the day you found out why".

PRESENT TIME

Many years later, when I met John de Ruiter, I soon
recognised that he had more of what I was seeking. I
learned that a beautiful experience is a gift: A gift to show
me something more profound. Generally, I want to
experience it more, or I want to experience it continually.
Experiencing it is not necessary because I already knew it.
Experiencing it more requires that I BECOME that profound
that I glimpsed; that I LIVE it. LIVING in that takes time, has
to be earned. John explained that an experience is like a
messenger; it brings me a message. I tend to look at the
messenger (the experience) more than the message (the bit of
newness that I can now see) then I want to meet the
messenger more.   My first awakening in 1966 showed
me that I am just a tiny, tiny spark of light, but it took a long,
long painful time to begin to understand or to sort it all out.
What great good fortune is mine to have found one, John de
Ruiter, who is all grown up in that!

PHILOSOPHICAL COMMENT

When the Light exploded on me, and I stood in the Light, I
thought of the Light as God, because I had been raised as a
Christian. If I had been raised as a Muslim I would have
thought of the Light as Allah. If I had been raised as a
Hindu, perhaps I would have thought of the Light as

Krishna. Or Atman? I would still have thought of it as a single entity, separate from me. But the awesome Light that I saw would still have been the same, and separation from IT would still have been a learned concept. If I had been raised as a non-believer, I would have...well, I would have become a believer, fast! But catching a glimpse of me as a speck of Light, as one of a thousand billion such specks, touched something deep in me that I began to realize only much later.

But I had a belief system in place; taught, learned, created and modified by me over the many years, to give me relief or comfort or self-protection in my experiences of life. Created to support what I liked or what I wanted to be true. My belief system created filters. A new experience had to run through my filters first, so I would interpret it accordingly. Thousands of people have reported profound experiences: Some big; some small. All are meaningful; precious. All are glimpses, and invitations to more. There's more. We're afraid to believe, afraid it would be too wonderful.

CHAPTER 2

ALONG THE WAY

TIMES PAST

Here are some of my experiences as I went stumbling along, making up my own story as I wandered through life; as I wandered away from HOME. (What's HOME? Is HOME where we came from?) If I seem to wander, and get tales mixed up in time---well, that's what old guys are supposed to do, isn't it?

When I graduated from High School (Dover, Ohio, 1948), the U S was drafting young men for 21 months service in the Army. It was random, so your Draft Board could call you anytime; or you might not get called at all. Every place I looked for a job they asked, "Have you served your time in the Army yet?" "No". "We can't hire you". Of course, I had been working part-time for over a year as a fireman at a brick yard. It was shift work; hot, gruelling work, shovelling coal into white-hot fire boxes, so I was looking for something better. I was looking for something full time, days, more permanent. But I could find none, so my best friend and I decided to enlist in the Air Force for four years. They sent me to Basic Training in San Antonio, Texas, for the summer.

It was hot. Then I was sent to school in Cheyenne, Wyoming, for the winter. It was cold and windy.

After school in Wyoming I was stationed at Goose Bay, Labrador, Canada, for the summer of 1949. I was working in the Cryptography Office. Since I had scored pretty high on my IQ test, my Section Chief came into the office one day and said, "Hagloch, get your hat, you're going to take a test for West Point." My response: "Get out of here! I don't want to go to West Point!" "Well, it wouldn't hurt to take the test," he said. So I got my hat, took off my gun belt (we wore a .45 side arm when on duty in the Crypto Office), and went to take the test. The results came in September; I passed. I could choose to return to the States, to an Army Prep School in New York State, or stay at Goose Bay. The mornings were getting nippy, and there were terrible stories abounding about winters at Goose Bay. There were stories about blizzards so bad that they would string a rope from the barracks to the mess hall, so you couldn't get lost before breakfast. Should I stay for a winter in Goose Bay? Or should I return to New York State and go to school? It seemed to me like a "no brainer"; so I chose to go South.

Most of the appointments into West Point are made by high-level politicians: Governors, Senators, Judges, etc. (They do their own screening; they don't send any dummies there.)

But a certain number of places in each class are reserved for competitive appointments from the Armed Services. So for nine months I attended a Prep School for West Point in New York State with men from the Air Force, Army, Navy and Marines. They were all pretty sharp guys.

We took the entrance tests in June 1950. I passed. In early July I got an Honorable Discharge from the Air Force and became inducted into the Army, and entered West Point.

We went through the Basic Training for the summer. It was rough. It is similar to Marine Basic Training (but from what I have heard, not as taxing physically). After about a month into classes in the fall, I began seriously thinking about where I was headed in my life. (If you were 21 years old, you COULD resign, and I had just turned 21.) The thought of an Army career for my life was very far from appealing. If I graduated from West Point I would receive a Regular Army Officer Commission. The decision to resign such a Commission sometime in the future would become almost impossible! "I'm headed in the wrong direction!" I thought. I resigned. I got an Honorable Discharge from the Army and went back to Ohio. My folks were very hurt. My Draft Board was mad, so they classified me 1-A, and eight months later sent me a Draft Notice! (They were drafting for 21 months in the Army; I had already spent 27 months in Service, and had two Honorable Discharges, but I had violated their rules.) By then I was married and my wife was pregnant. I re-enlisted in the Air Force for four more years. We moved to Oklahoma (my oldest daughter was born as an "Okie"); then to Georgia; and then I got orders to go to Korea (just after the Armistice was signed in '53).

When I came back from Korea (1954) I was stationed in Northern California. I was Air Force, but I was attached to an Army Engineers Battalion. So I learned to drive trucks, tractors, rollers, graders and bulldozers. The benefits? 1. I learned to drive heavy equipment (which I loved). 2. I got my fill of military life, so I determined to go to college as soon as I got out. 3. I lived in California, so I was determined to return there as soon as I was through college. (I earned a Bachelor of Science degree in Aeronautical Engineering; then I got a job offer in San Diego. Bingo! I was in the" Space Race".)

I earned pretty good grades in College, so I had a number of interviews for jobs, including a visit and interview at Los Alamos, New Mexico. Los Alamos, on a high plateau, was the research centre which designed the first atomic bombs: the first for the Trinity Test in July 1945; the second called Little Boy, dropped over Hiroshima 20 days later; the third called Fat Man, dropped over Nagasaki in another three days. These actions were viewed by many as a disaster and an atrocity, while others argued that millions of lives were saved by ending the war suddenly. After all my interviews I was offered more money to stay in the East, but one offer from San Diego did it. It was "California-or-Bust" for us.

I went to work for the Astronautics Division of Convair in San Diego in the spring of 1958. They built the Atlas Launch Vehicle (powered by liquid oxygen and jet fuel), and the Centaur high energy upper stage (powered by liquid oxygen and liquid hydrogen). At first, I was assigned to the Trajectory Design Group, working on the Atlas ICBM (Inter-Continental Ballistic Missile) Program. Convair had been awarded the first contract for that kind of a system. I computed trajectories from several launch points in the U S to all significant targets in Russia and China. Later, when the Atlas System was replaced in the field by the second-generation system, most of those Atlases were used for space launch experiments. So I worked on a number of NASA and Air Force space programs. Later I became a Project Engineer over the technical areas of Trajectory Design, Guidance, Aerodynamics, Thermodynamics and Range Safety Studies.

I worked on two pre-Apollo test programs. One was named "FIRE". (Ref. 1). It was a test of the adequacy of the ceramic heat shield on the Apollo spacecraft during re-entry into Earth's atmosphere. In each flight the test package—a

miniature Apollo spacecraft with a solid rocket attached —
was launched from Cape Canaveral in Florida. As it
approached re-entry west of South Africa, the solid rocket
was ignited to drive the test vehicle into the atmosphere at
37,000 feet per second. When you are in low Earth orbit your
speed is about 25,000 feet per second (five miles per second)
(seven and a half kilometers per second). To re-enter you
slow down a bit and re-enter at near 25,000 feet per second.
(Ref. 2). When you return from the Moon your re-entry
speed is about 37,000 feet per second (12 times the speed of a
rifle bullet). (Ref.3).

Meteoroids enter the atmosphere at speeds in the order of
40,000 feet per second, and faster. (Can be much faster.) They
become "shooting stars" and burn up.

The heat shield on the saucer-shaped, or shallow bowl-
shaped, leading edge of Apollo was covered with ceramic. It
takes a lot of heat to melt ceramic. Atmospheric ram-
pressure and friction heat up the ceramic to the liquid state,
and it flows off the edges as red-hot molten ceramic. That's
how the heat is dissipated or carried away.

The first test flight of the FIRE Program produced less than
perfect results. The spent rocket case, which somewhat
resembled an empty piece of stove pipe, was backed away

from the mini-Apollo spacecraft by a small retro rocket. But the empty rocket case was running in the wake of the spacecraft where the atmospheric air pressure was near zero behind a Mach-25-Plus shock wave so it didn't slow down as quickly as the spacecraft, and it passed the spacecraft. This messed up some of the test results: Photography, telemetry, etc. There were meetings and brain-storming sessions on how to fix the problem for the second flight. They decided that we could add one more retro rocket (about the impulse of a rifle cartridge) without exceeding weight limits. The Air Force owned a computer program (I think it was called *A Six-Degree-of-Freedom* Program) that could track, or compute the trajectories of two vehicles in proximity as they re-entered the atmosphere; how they interacted as air drag slowed them down. They made the program available to me, to do a trajectory study. After running a few dozen trajectories, with the second retro rocket pointing in different directions and fired at different times, I told them to mount it cross-wise. They were quite surprised; 'Oh! Really?' but when I presented the results of the study they were convinced. The cross-wise impulse tumbled the empty rocket case and kicked it outside the wake of the spacecraft, so it slowed down much faster than the spacecraft. The second flight was a great success. The miniature Apollo re-entered at 37,000 feet per second, survived, and provided a mountain of data.

The second pre-Apollo program I worked on was the Gemini Program. To land a man on the Moon we (explorers from Earth) needed to put a spacecraft in orbit around the Moon, send a smaller craft down to the Moon surface, blast the smaller craft back up from the Moon, and rendezvous with the craft in orbit. Then the two could fire up and return to Earth. Rendezvous in orbit is a very delicate maneuver. It had never been done before. The Gemini Program was generated to learn rendezvous in space. (Of course, in recent years it is used extensively. Spacecraft routinely rendezvous with the International Space Station.) Rendezvous requires precise timing. If the target craft is moving at 25,000 feet per second, you can't be two seconds late (or early); you'd miss by 50,000 feet (ten miles). If you're off by ten miles you can't just drive over there. You have to change your velocity vector by a few feet per second so that, 90 minutes later, when you've completed an orbit around the earth, you'll be closer. In the Gemini Program our involvement at Convair happened because the contractor who was to launch the Gemini Target into low Earth orbit was late; they couldn't meet the schedule. NASA approached Convair with a query: Can you put the Gemini Target into orbit in 30 days? Ordinarily a test program would take 18 months from inception to launch. Convair's answer: Yes, we can. Management of the project was handled by a Program Manager and 15 Project Engineers, each handling a technical part of the project. I was a Project Engineer covering the areas of Trajectory Design, Guidance, Aerodynamics, Thermodynamics and Range Safety Studies (as on Program FIRE). The team met very early, before the start of the work day, every morning. We did it.

I never dreamed of being an astronaut myself, but I met some. America's first men in space (the Mercury Program) were launched into orbit by Atlas vehicles. I didn't work on the Mercury Program, but the man at the desk next to mine did the trajectory design work for launch and power into orbit, so several of those astronauts were in our office often talking to him. They wanted to talk to the man charting the flights of the rockets they would ride. They were some pretty sharp guys; they didn't miss a jot nor a tittle.

CHAPTER 3

SHOCK WAVE

TIMES PAST

Then, in 1966, I had that awesome awakening that I described in Chapter 1. Within a couple of days after that experience I realized that my views and opinions on just about everything in life were no longer valid. My understanding was changing. I became extremely interested in reading the Bible. I would spontaneously wake up about 4 a.m. each morning and read for a couple of hours before I had to get ready for work in the "space race". This went on for about three years, and during that time I read the Old Testament through, cover to cover, three times; and the New Testament about eight times. Each morning I would read a while in the Old Testament and a while in the New. In each I started at the beginning and read straight through to the end; and then started over at the beginning again. I found it so interesting! I was starting to think that life is not the way I'd been picturing it, and working it out. It is not that way at all! There's more.

PHILOSOPHICAL COMMENT

When a prophet or a sage or a seer or a teacher of Truth (if indeed he be a person of true beingness of *reality)* proclaims a Truth, it is true; it is created. We may have to listen to it being spoken many, many, many times before we begin to hear it. But it was true all along. The words might fly past our dull ears a thousand times (or a thousand generations) before it is heard. But they were true and real all along.

I read that Jesus said, "...you are all god..." In reading the New Testament over and over I found that to be the deepest teaching of Jesus. "...You are all god..." Book of John 10:34. ("...you are gods..." RSV Ref. 5); ("...you are god(s)..." KJV Ref. 6); ("...ye are Elohim..." Restoration of Original Sacred Name Bible Ref. 7). Many translations added the 's' to make it plural because the translators were so locked into the concept of separateness that they could not comprehend the idea in the singular. In my initial awakening glimpse, I saw no separation. "You are all Elohim." Essence of god. God stuff. Made of that. I belong. Way back I began to get a little glimpse of that, but didn't understand. I had been thoroughly indoctrinated with the common concept of the World that God is a separate entity way up there and I am a separate remote person way down here. So, my indoctrination quickly covered-over what Jesus said. An inkling of a glimpse of that reality lingered somewhere in the back of my mind; so, I was always looking for more. As long as I see myself separate, and identify as a separate "myself", it's impossible to get the meaning, the profound significance, of what Jesus said.

PRESENT TIME

Not until I met John de Ruiter and he started inviting me HOME, showing me that I could return HOME, did the possibility of really seeing it begin to open up. I learned, and came to realize, that what I really am is a tiny little bit of IT, of HOME. That I was born into this world as that. I realized that I had left HOME. So, I had to change my concept of God. My concept, inherited from previous generations, and taught by all my teachers, preachers and advisers, didn't match what Jesus said. It placed God separate and out of reach, and me separate with no way to be with God. Why did that seem to be opposite from what Jesus said?

When John de Ruiter teaches that we are all deep inside at the foundation of our existence, we are tiny bits of It, of the Source of Life, and he invites us to return HOME; he is not initiating some new radical teaching. He is opening up and bringing to the forefront knowledge which was established of ancient times.

"You are all Elohim." I never heard that concept mentioned, nor even hinted at, in any of the Christian churches or circles that I ever encountered. The idea that each of us was born into this world as a tiny little piece of IT; of God stuff. (All seven billion of us.)

PHILOSOPHICAL COMMENT

Elohim: One of the names of the profound in the Hebrew language – along with YAW and YAWVAH. They probably always thought of it as a remote, separate being, way up there, but it wasn't. It was always also within. They probably always thought of themselves as alone; but they were not...They were always tiny parts of It. Even in Genesis, the first book of the Bible, it doesn't speak of It as a separate identity, for the wording is "...Let us make man in our image..." (Gen 1:26 Ref. 6). And in verse 27 "So God created man in his own image". Or, in the original Hebrew, "And Elohim created man in his own image..." (Ref. 7). So, man has always been **of God.** People are, and always were, tiny bits of the source of Life, MEANING.

Jesus taught in parables. The Upanishads (considered to be based on direct knowledge of God, reference 8) of the Hindu stream of philosophy/religion/belief taught in a similar manner around 500 years earlier. The Bhagavad Gita (Ref. 8) about 100 years earlier. The Bhagavad Gita expresses the realization that the Presence is manifested in every life, and no life is separated from It. That the real purpose of life is to discover this and to realize God while living here on Earth.

We've always spoken of Jesus as the Son of God, but he always spoke of himself as the son of man. Did he do this perhaps to emphasize, to make plain, to clarify that we are Elohim? That we are all the same at the foundation of our existence? Both always have been and always will be real. I can accept, respond; I can like that.

All my experiences of a profound nature are not unique. I've read many books and talked to many people who have had wonderful, eye-opening, life-changing experiences. My experiences are not something special. Meeting John de Ruiter is.

The way I understand (at the present time) my life in the bigger picture is: I was conceived and born into this world as a pure, clean, innocent, incorruptible, indefatigable being, little bit of IT; of MEANING. The reality of this has been prophetically established in the foundations of the major religious belief systems. I was HOME. I came into an environment filled with the concept of separateness. I came up clothed with the sludge of this age (we all were). What's the sludge? The idea, the concept, the belief that we are separate. The pressure to conform to the world-wide concept that we are separate was overwhelming. All my forefathers, and all my friends and their forefathers, and all my teachers and their forefathers were thoroughly entrenched in this concept. So, I gradually left HOME and bought into the belief system of the world. I identified with the sludge. I became a sludge-bunny. This belief system contains many great ideas for a guy like me: I'm my own boss; I belong to me; I can strive to make anything I want to of myself; I can live my life my way; I'm a sovereign individual. These are all lucrative ideas; I bought in. So, I separated from my Source. I left HOME. I became a sludge-bunny. (I really always was a God-baby; but I pictured myself as a sludge-bunny.)

Sludge: Not a nice-sounding word. How does the Webster's dictionary define it? 1. Mud, mire, or ooze; slush. 2. A mud-like deposit, especially sediment produced during the treatment of sewerage. How am I using it? The teaching, the belief, the concept, the doctrine imposed upon us down through the ages and generations that we are separate and alone. That's not real. We are not sludge-bunnies. Deep inside and hidden, covered by layers of teaching, we are God-babies.

Doctor Mary Neal, in her spectacular book "To Heaven and Back", (Ref. 9) wrote on several occasions that she realized that little children still remembered "God's World". That caught my attention. Did I remember what I was when I was very young? Did I make a point of "not remembering"? Did I do that to make certain that I would not remember "God's World"? Every experience (and I've had many) was an invitation to return. Had I become an expert at tossing out invitations with the junk mail? John explains that deep down inside we all remember "God's world"; it's the foundation of our existence; we've just learned how to cover it over and bury it so deep into our subconscious selves that we can't see it. Why did we all forget?

Kittens open their eyes in two or three days. As children of the world, as world babies, do we close our eyes in two or three or four years?

"...you were born in sin," you have to do something. It seems to me that perhaps I could just stop "doing something"; stop doing what I'm doing to maintain my status away from HOME. Stop building up a "myself" as I have been doing all these years. Stop maintaining a difference between Real me and myself.

I was raised believing that I was born separate from God: "You were born in sin; you must..." I gradually found out that that idea was not true. I finally realized that what Jesus taught is the opposite of that. He said that we are all Elohim. I finally realized that we are born into this world as pure, clean, tiny bits of the Source, of all that is real. We come up into a world that is thoroughly indoctrinated with the idea of separateness. We come up coated with sludge...the idea of separation. I didn't need to accept the wayward teaching, but I did (everybody was doing it). Realizing the difference enables us to return HOME --- to personally identify as what we really are. That's the word that Jesus spoke to the best, most learned religious leaders of His day: "...you are all god..." We all come into the realm of Earth as little pieces of Reality: All seven billion of us. We are each a little bit of It. If we were not that, we wouldn't have life.

From the Book of John (Ref. 7), starting at 10:30, "I and the Father are one. The Jews again lifted up stones that they might stone Him. YAHSHUA answered them, "many works have I showed you, noble ones from My Father: for which of those works are ye stoning Me? The Jews answered Him, concerning a noble work are we not stoning Thee; but concerning profane speech, and because Thou, being a man, art making Thyself Elohim. YAHSHUA answered them, is it not written in your law: I said, Ye are Elohim?" He was quoting from the Prophet recorded in Psalms 82:6 "I said, Elohim ye are, yea, sons of the Highest are ye all." So, the reality of this has been prophetically established in the foundations of Christianity and Judaism. "...the basic theological concepts of Islam are virtually identical with those of Judaism and Christianity, its forerunners." (Ref. 10). "The Koran honors Jesus as a prophet, and accepts his virgin birth..." (Ref. 10). So, this knowledge of Reality is also established in the foundation of their faith. As I read the Quran, (Ref. 13), especially in Heifer 136, I understand that the followers of the Muslim faith accept and embrace the teaching given through Abraham, Isaac, Ishmael, Jacob, Moses, Jesus and the other prophets in the Hebrew stream of belief. So, the proclamation that we are all of God and one with the Source of All is embedded deep in the foundation of their belief. The Hindu religion, the oldest of the religions, voiced this truth also; that man consists of three parts ... body, the personality, the Divine. Houston Smith in his study of the world's religions (Ref. 10) points out that the basic teaching of Hinduism is that man consists of three basic parts: Body, Personality and Atman-Brahman. The Atman-Brahman part, the hidden part, is the eternal part, but covered over by the teachings of the world, by the desire to be in control and direct our surface lives. Buried under sludge.

PRESENT TIME

So, the knowledge of this Reality is embedded in the foundations of the major religious belief systems. Most of the many far eastern religions are expansions and additions to the original Hindu belief system. But we are rapidly taught to believe other things and stuff. The Truth has been over-ridden by much teachings. Religions take something which has a resonance of truth and build much structure (thoughts, concepts, reasoning) around it. The structures all serve a sovereign "myself" identity. I found a man who not only caught on, but fully embraced it, and who is able to teach me, lead me, guide me to return to the knowledge of Reality. His name is John de Ruiter. Is he special? If someone has reached into more than we've reached into we have a tendency to consider that one special. John says that he is just being what we all actually are deep inside; but he is all grown up in it, as it. He's inviting us HOME. He was called: He answered. Actually, he's a leader, a front-runner, who shows us what we all can be. He's a door into the unknown; into the possibility. Jesus opened the door a crack; the Upanishads opened the door a crack; the Bhagavad Gita opened the door a crack; John is opening it wide, inviting entrance. Something new of Reality was initiated more than 2000 years ago; now, in these days, it is being opened up, developed, made plain and brought to fruition.

So the Truth was spoken, though there may be no ears that will hear it, nor hearts that will respond. But the Truth always remained true. But here and there, down through history, there was an occasional ear that heard, and an open heart that responded, and little steps were taken. Then Jesus came, and made a big change. And now, John de Ruiter.

In one meeting a woman was questioning John, and during the conversation it came out that Jesus has appeared to him thousands of times and taught him and imparted to him all that he is and all that he teaches and all that he does. The woman asked," Well! When was the last time He appeared to you?" John was silent for a long minute, and then said," Right now." I was riding home with a friend, a psychic, who had been a psychic since she was a little girl, since way before she knew what the word meant. (She was so sensitive that she could pick up radar over the hill, and slow down.) She could see energy patterns, and she would sit and watch John's energy pattern: How he moved, how his energy pattern responded. She was also very familiar with Jesus' energy pattern. She said that when the woman asked the question, "When was the last time He appeared to you?" Jesus' energy pattern appeared behind John's---and melted into him. And then he said, "right now." That was just one of many little experiences that helped me to realize, to clarify, to solidify, who John is, what he is, what he is being, from where he is living, and from where he is inviting us to return HOME.

John explained that Jesus would come to him and show him something new and go away and not return until John was walking in that little bit of newness. And Jesus laid His mantle on John's shoulders: To prepare a people; to bring a people in. The way I think of it Jesus said something like, "Okay, John, you've got the ball, run with it. Call a people; lead a people forth; bring a people into what's next. Rake the fields, scour the high places, shake the bushes; a few good souls will tumble out. A few soft and open hearts will respond. A few tender hearts will step forward. A remnant, a few happy, free people, will walk with you. A few hungry ears will hear."

PHILOSOPHICAL COMMENT

When Jesus came the first time He sent His servant before Him, to prepare the way: John the Baptist. The story of John the Baptist is presented in Matthew 3, Mark 1, the first few chapters of Luke and John 1. (When I was visiting Israel, I soaked my feet in the River Jordan at the place where it is said that John the Baptist baptized Jesus. Nice.)

If someone is exhibiting more than we've reached into, our natural tendency is to exalt that one, to think of that one as "big". (Alternately we might scoff and say, 'who does he make himself out to be?') Might we consider "little" instead of "big"? Could it be that that one is little enough to reach into more than I have reached into? Small enough, surrendered enough, soft enough, open enough to respond to a calling? To answer a call? When Paul wrote of Apostles (I'll explain more in Chapter 7) he wasn't describing them as being considered big, exalted, but rather as "...the scum of the earth."

PRESENT TIME

What is HOME? I had a little glimpse of one aspect of it. John took me there. In my experience I was moving at great speed. As in the movies of "Star Trek", when they went to Warp speed, the stars were whizzing by as streaks of light, and then, suddenly, it all stopped. I was in total blackness. Deep, dark quietness. No light. No movement. Nothing. I thought, "It's SO quiet." Total peace. HOME. Incredibly quiet! Unimaginable profound peace. Deep black: Where everything comes from… EVERYTHING. I know it because I've been there. When it moves there is light, awesome brilliant light; I know because I've seen the light. It moves as love; I know because I've felt the love---I've wallowed in the love. Unimaginable love. Love beyond love. Dr. Eben Alexander, in his second book, "The Map of Heaven" (Ref.11) reported a similar experience. He wrote "I ascended until I reached the core, that deepest *sanctum sanctorum* of the Divine --- infinite inky blackness, filled to overflowing with indescribable, unconditional love."

When John took me in to the black, there was nothing: no light, total black, no movement. It was so quiet, so peaceful, so serene. John explained that when Reality is not moving there is total blackness, (I understood) and as it moves there is light. It moves as love. Its movement is love and light, sometimes an explosion of light. What term or word should I use to describe the black? Shall I say It? Or Life? Or the Source? Or Reality? Or God? In my thinking now, the least useful of these terms is the word God. Why? Because in this world of religions there has been so much teachings about God and gods. Employing that term immediately sets our thoughts in a direction. It directs our minds toward a concept of a Being or beings higher than us, remote, separate from us. It sets our minds spinning. This direction precludes the concept of Reality – the Black. So, we've shut out the possibility of seeing that we are all of that; that we are one; that we belong. In that direction of thought we are turned away; we left HOME. Then we cannot see what we really are. I had to replace the word "God" in the vocabulary of my thinking with something more conducive to letting me see Reality. John uses the word Meaning; that's better. The Big Picture is a lot bigger than I imagined it to be.

Getting ready for bed one night (June '05) I looked at myself in the mirror. To my great surprise and very great shock I was looking into the eyes of God. But it was my own eyes I was looking into. Whether I would interpret it as the eyes of

God, or the eyes of the Profound, or the Source, or MEANING, or the eyes of real me, or John----it doesn't matter. I KNEW! It was very pronounced and very strong and very real. I was IT. Very clearly, I could see that I belong. Very clearly, I could see that I am *of* God. (Not as if I were *the one; but rather that I am made of the same stuff*.) My first reaction was, 'No! That's too big!' So, I tried to deny it, but it was definitely undeniable. I remember trying to deny it three times; hard! But it was completely and definitely undeniable! IT COULD NOT BE DENIED! So, I went to bed. That's me. That's real me. Is this part of Post HOME Development? Was I able to cover it over for a few more years? I'm realizing that as a very little boy I learned to cover over what I knew of "God's World" (as Mary Neal put it), and make my own way away from HOME. And I've had decades of perfecting my technique of covering it over. Of shoving what I knew so far into the background that I couldn't see it. I'd become an expert at covering-it-over. I'm an expert "cover-up-er". Why would I want to do that? Could it be that I don't want the responsibility that goes along with such knowing? I remember once, a long time ago, John de Ruiter asked me, "Do you know who you are?" I answered, "I know who YOU are, and that's enough." He said, "That's NOT enough; you have to know who YOU are." I need to know what I am. I need to know THAT I AM.

Later I had that remarkable glimpse of seeing that I AM!
We're afraid to believe; afraid it would be too wonderful.

PHILOSOPHICAL COMMENT

If I could let go of everything (my life history, my "story"),
what would be left would be only Reality. One cannot drop
Reality---it's real. If I could drop my attitudes, the
judgements I've formed because of life experiences, my
conclusions about life, my belief system, my moral code, etc.,
etc., ---I'd be back where I left Home---a very little kid. We
are each a very little bit of IT. If we were not that, we
wouldn't have life. I think that nobody can entirely leave
Home. We always remember something of 'God's World'.
We always retain some knowledge of the Goodness. There's
always some relating to that Goodness. We came from
Home; we return to Home when we die; by trying to get
away from Home during our short times we have in the
body here on Earth, do we only forfeit a unique and
awesome opportunity to develop some measure of Reality?

"If you are interested in Truth, then there will not be a path
at all. If Truth is all you really want, just so that you can give
yourself to it, then there is an immediate surrender within: a
total surrender of all that you are doing and all that you
have acquired for yourself in being a 'somebody', and there
is a simple resting in consciousness within. That rest from

striving and doing for self-created agendas is you as consciousness finally residing in a way of being that is true. It is you as consciousness returning 'home'." Quoted from John's first book, "Unveiling Reality" (Ref.12.)

Consider this silly little scenario: It's olden times and it's very dark and very foggy, and people can see only five meters. A man comes along claiming to see ten meters. People get together to determine what to do about him. They reach an agreement: "Let's kill him; he's crazy; because everybody knows it's impossible to see farther than five meters." In time - years - the fog lifts a little, and average people can see ten meters. Along comes one who says he can see 25 meters. People decide to kill him (because he's crazy; everyone knows you can see only ten meters). This has been going on for thousands of generations. Later another comes along who claims to see 100 meters; what do we do with him? Kill. (Of course, after we kill his body he can probably see 1000 meters.) We don't need to fear seeing farther into Reality. Were veils being slowly lifted over a long, long time? We're afraid to believe; afraid it would be too wonderful.

A change is coming; how fast it comes, we can't see yet. If I'm away from Home and, therefore, using only a small fraction of my mental capability (say 5 percent) ---to make my decisions, to plan my life, to form my attitudes and conclusions and judgements, to learn of myself and others and the world and the universe, to evaluate reality----- I wonder: What does the other 95 percent of Reality looks like? It was not that many generations back in time when everyone KNEW that the Earth was flat.

We humans are a curious lot. We have a great need to understand. We want to know "what-is-it?" And engineers and scientists want to know not only "what-is-it?" but "how-much-of-what-is-it?" We have many questions about "What is God?" If I could understand, if I could wrap my head around God, would that make me one size bigger than It? Can I really let go of my 'story'? I've spent all these years creating it, developing it, expanding it. I kind of cling to it. I understand that when I die my whole 'story' goes poof! like a puff of smoke on a summer breeze. When I lose the body, my game is over. When I die (check out, pass on, croak, perish, become extinct, buy the farm, cash in my chips, find myself without breath, kick the bucket, push up grass, push up daisies, peg out, become defunct, draw the curtains, take the big sleep, blink for an exceptionally long time, sign off, terminate, shuffle off this mortal plain, take the last breath, cross over, pay my debt to nature) it's all gone anyway.

PRESENT TIME

John de Ruiter once said that we, on an average, (maintaining our status away from Home) use only about 3 percent of our actual mental capability. Richard Panek in his book "The 4% Universe; Dark Matter, Dark Energy, and the Race to Discover the Root of Reality" (Ref. 15) described in great detail the years of research in the disciplines of Photometry, Astronomy, Spectroscopy, Cosmology, Physical Cosmology, Particle Physics and Particle Astrophysics, with much cooperation amongst the many groups. His book is called "The Inside Story of the 2011 Nobel Prize in Physics". The prize was awarded to Saul Pearlmutter, Brian Schmitt and Adam Riess. After a seven-year intense study by people of those groups, a conclusion was reached that we see and know less than 5% of our universe. That the universe consists of 72.8% dark energy, 22.7% of dark matter, and only 4.56% of baryonic matter. Baryonic matter means all of the stuff (air, water, rocks, plants, our bodies, planets, stars...everything that we can see and define). The 95.44%, dark energy and dark matter is completely unknown. They concluded that the study was a "precise accounting of the depth of our ignorance." (Ref. 15). If we see and comprehend only 4.56 percent of our lives and our universe, I wonder, what does the other 95.44% look like? I guess if we can see only that little bit it doesn't make us very big, wise, nor in command.

But inside I seem to have a demand to know, to understand. Why? If I'm using only about 5 % of my mental capacity, (actually about 4.56 percent) can't I just accept that I am unable to understand the big picture? Can't I accept that I don't NEED to understand anyway? Isn't my inside demand just silly?

A person was questioning John, complaining about all the trials and hardships that we must endure in our lives. "It's so unfair, why would God make me suffer so much?" I had a thought, if I were God, I would design it more fairly. Then I thought, hey Ralphie, hey sludge-bunny, if you're able to use only about 5% of your brain and able to perceive a maximum 4.56% of the universe, do you really feel qualified to design the Big Picture? To design the Universe? To set the rules of life? Maybe you should just accept what is; roll with the punches of this life, and be open and soft about it. Be at rest with John. I could *like* being open and soft.

PHILOSOPHICAL COMMENT

Since we actually are tiny, tiny pieces of the Source, we are genius, we are real swift puppies, we can know what John is and look down our noses at those who don't know, we can know what John is and work our agendas around that. We cannot really know what John is and have a soft open heart toward what we think he is. We can have a real dedication to follow him…what we think he is. We can be real religious about either position I have described, or any level of knowing or understanding between the two. Probably each person has a different or unique level of knowing or understanding him. So, it is not about knowing or seeing or being called or understanding that is key, it is openness and softness of heart that is key. It is honesty to the core that is key, the Source moves as love; if it moves through me it moves as love. I can *like* being open and soft.

PRESENT TIME

Dr. Eben Alexander, in his book "Proof of Heaven", (Ref. 16) wrote of his truly wonderful experience of dying and going to Heaven for a little while. What an invitation! I see that, as Reality moves, such an experience is now becoming available before dying. I can shift my orientation from identifying as myself to identifying as the Truth that I know in my heart. I'm seeing the opportunity of manifesting this Truth, MEANING. Is this what I was born for? Is it answering a Calling? Is this Post Home Development? I can continually keep my heart open for more.

John de Ruiter gave me that glimpse of HOME. He took me there: Deep, totally dark, quiet, no movement, complete peace, no light. Inexplicable peace. Peace beyond peace. He explains and shows us that we actually have access to and can live in other realms. He lives in other realms; he comes from other realms. How can we….? Openness and softness of heart; kindness; okayness; response to what we actually KNOW deep inside.

I was visiting a friend and he offered me a cookie; home made, chocolate chip; very desirable. He handed me a narrow-necked, half-gallon jar half full of cookies. I figured that I could squeeze my hand into the jar if my hand was open and my fingers sort of scrunched together. But if my fingers were wrapped around a cookie, I could never exit. I said, "It's a monkey trap, right"? We both laughed. I had read somewhere that that's one way you might catch a monkey. You make available a narrow-necked jar with the monkey's favorite food inside. He could get his hand in, open, but clutching the food he could not withdraw it. If he wouldn't let go of the food, you had him.

PHILOSOPHICAL COMMENT

Myself, as I've created it, is a monkey trap???

I see where I want to go---HOME. It's very desirable. I can see the door: It's very small. Real me could squeeze through, easily. Myself is too big. I get right up to the door with myself in hand. If I would open my hand I could go through. But with my hand closed over myself---no go. I reach; but one hand is still stuck in the cookie jar. Is wanting to feel it all the time like putting my hand into the cookie jar? Myself can change; I could grow up. I could let myself gradually learn to become a manifestation of Elohim. Is that big? No; I think that's little. Very tiny. Smaller than I have always wanted to be.

PRESENT TIME

I was sitting home alone one day and sort of fretting inside because I knew what I wanted to be but stuck in "myself" I couldn't. I saw myself standing before a rock wall with a tiny hole in it. Then suddenly I popped through and I could see me as a little sphere, very dark, sailing through the black. The vision, or knowing concept, stayed for several hours, slowly fading.

CHAPTER 4

SEARCHING

TIMES PAST

Back in late 1967, with the ups-and-downs in the Aerospace
Industry, I was laid off. After my unemployment checks ran
out I drove taxi for a year.

After my spectacular, brief encounter with the Light, I went
through many, many months of "deep soul-searching". The
excitement of working in the "space race" was waning
compared to what I was beginning to be aware of in other
realms; knowing that there is a vast world that I'm not in. I'd
had a glimpse; but how could I get into it? I was getting
more and more desperate to find it; to stand in the Light
again. I had seen something vast, wonderful, different; it
matters more than life.

In my searching I attended meetings of a small Charismatic
group for several years. It was started by a retired
Pentecostal preacher who had received the Baptism in the
Holy Spirit. He was acquainted with many preachers, from
different Denominations, who had received the Baptism in
the Holy Spirit and spoke in tongues. (Many had been

kicked out of their churches because of it.) So he invited a different Spirit-filled preacher to speak each week. Their messages were about Holy Spirit baptism, speaking in tongues, healing and getting healed. I experienced all of those. (I think that the first outbreak of speaking in tongues in modern times occurred in a small church in Los Angeles in 1906. "William J. Seymour, a black hotel waiter, soon took the Pentecostal message and carried it to Los Angeles, where a revival broke out at Azusa Street in 1906." (Ref. 4).) Being in a charismatic movement was helpful. It was a good stepping stone; not a good parking place.

One week the speaker was a Spirit-filled Catholic Priest. After the meeting we were invited to come to him for a blessing with the "laying-on-of-hands". I went. A young woman was ministering with him, and she was hearing a voice which she (and the Priest) believed was God speaking to her. As the Priest prayed for me with his hands on my head, the woman stood beside me praying softly in tongues with her fingertips, trembling, resting lightly on my shoulder. After the prayer the woman asked me, "Are you some kind of a preacher?" I said "No". The Priest asked the woman, "Why? What did He say to you?" The woman answered the Priest, "He said, 'he's an Apostle'." They were both perplexed, dumbfounded. Me, too. I didn't know what they were talking about. I left, and drove home, about five miles. I was so high that I felt that I had to hang onto the steering wheel to stay down. I was still perplexed, but knowing that there's more. Lots more. We're afraid to believe; afraid it would be too wonderful.

PHILOSOPHICAL COMMENT

What's an Apostle? The twelve who walked with Jesus were called Apostles. So was Paul, who dramatically met Jesus later, on the road to Damascus. From what I had learned in church circles, an Apostle was one who was (is) intimate with the Lord. John Robert Stevens was known as an apostle. Did my awakening in '66 qualify? Certainly not in my thinking.

What is God? John de Ruiter said, "God is the being of all space." I thought: Every rock, every flower, every blade of grass, every animal, every mountain, every drop of water, every molecule of air, every person, every bug, every star. Me, too. (But this was already proclaimed and taught in the Hindu Upanishads and the Bhagavad Gita more than 2000 years earlier.) Each one of us is a little piece of It, the Source, God, MEANING! Wow! That HAS to be more magnificent than me myself living alone in my own little self-created box, trying to look up. I found that my learned concept of God was far too small. I've revised my vocabulary somewhat. I've replaced the word God with IT, or Source, or Truth, or

MEANING. One teacher calls it LIFE. Using that word, "God," immediately brings up a concept of a Being remote and separate from us. I shouldn't use the word "God" at all, because it triggers the world-wide concept, held by all religious belief systems throughout history, of a Being (or beings) of higher power, separate from us. That's not true. This introduces an error in understanding, an error in communication, as the foundation for consideration or discussion. Since Reality is not like that, we've started with a block on ability to stretch our understanding into new, more real territory. We need to use some word, or words, other than "God." It took a long time for me to understand (although the knowing of it was there in what I saw in my first awakening) that my concept of God did not conform to Reality. It took a long time to gradually comprehend that my God was too small. I had been opened up to the Light. I had stood in Its awesome presence. I had instantly recognized It as God…my learned concept of God. My concept of God was inadequate. My learned idea of what God is was far, FAR too small! What term might we employ to describe Reality? It? Life? Meaning? Essence? God? The Apostle John, author of the fourth book of the New Testament of the Bible, got a glimpse of it; he used "The Word." "In the beginning was the Word, and the Word was with God, and the Word was God. He was in the beginning with God; (Jn 1:1-2, Ref. 5). Then in verse 14 "And the Word became flesh and dwelt among us…" Perhaps the least useful of all these terms is "God", because it immediately throws our thinking into the idea or concept of a Being remote from us; the world-wide concept of separation from the foundation of our Life. Then we're spinning.

PRESENT TIME

When John de Ruiter said, God is the being of all space, I connected that with some things I had read in the "Restoration of Sacred Name Bible," (Ref. 7). When Moses saw the burning bush and turned aside and received the commission to return to Egypt: In Exodus 3, "And Moses said unto Elohim, Lo! as surely as I go in unto the sons of Israel, and say unto them, The Elohim of your fathers hath sent me unto you, so surely they will say unto me, What is His name? And Elohim said unto Moses, I Will Become whatsoever I please, and He said, thus shalt thou say to the sons of Israel, I Will Become hath sent me unto you. And Elohim said yet further unto Moses, thus shalt thou say unto the sons of Israel, YAHVAH, Elohim of your fathers, Elohim of Abraham, Elohim of Isaac and Elohim of Jacob hath sent me unto you. This is My name to times age-abiding, and this My memorial to generation after generation." (Ex 3:13-15, Ref. 7). And in the introductory notes to that translation: "EHYAH ASHER EHYEH. Literally, "I will be that I will be," Ex. iii. 14. But as the so-called future or long tense expresses not simply the FUTURE, but also and especially CONTINUANCE, the force is, "I continue to be, and will be, what I continue to be, and will be."" (Page XIV of Ref. 7). And "..."Extol Him that rideth upon the heavens" (or the void spaces of infinitude) "by His name JAH" (the eternal One), "and rejoice before Him." The word for heavens here is not the usual word, but a word expressive of desolateness---space untenanted and void. Infinitude and eternity are indwelt by Him." Page XIV of Ref. 7). All that made sense to me and rang true. Everything that is is a manifestation of It, of Meaning. Me, too. Coming back Home is responding to that.

PHILOSOPHICAL COMMENT

I can think of it as It, or God, or the Source, or etc. One teacher I heard calls it LIFE. Dr. Alexander (Ref.11) calls it "Om" because that was the humming sound he heard. John refers to it as Meaning. The concept introduced in the "Star Wars" movies was "The Force." It grows where it may. God does not channel. Life, the Source, Meaning, God, grows and expands where it may. It flows through itself. It cannot flow through what is not its own to grow in a secondary place. It does not channel. Christ does not create Christ through one who is not of Him; who is not His. That would be like a twig or a branch separating from its tree, floating out 6 or 7 feet in mid air and the tree trying to grow leaves on it. Silly.

MEANING. It flows where it may; wherever it finds a soft and open heart; wherever there is acceptance, surrender.

Employing the terms of Ref. 7, everywhere that the Source, Meaning, is manifested, El is manifested; and everywhere It is manifested in human form is Elohim. I can choose to let it grow and manifest in me; or I have the creative capability to turn my back and manufacture my own "story" of my life. All my life I did the latter---until I met John de Ruiter.

Of course, it is easy to disregard all of this; to not believe it; to throw it all out. I did so myself once, a long time ago. But that was before I met the Light. How open am I to receive or embrace new concepts? We're afraid to believe...afraid it would be too wonderful.

PRESENT TIME

Sometimes, when John walks into a room I get tuned into him, to what he is being inside. I find him so open, so soft, so surrendered inside...I cry.

Sometimes, when I meet face-to-face with John I can immediately, instantly, see the gap between what he is being and what I am being. My tendency is to look at my end of the gap. That is being identified in myself, as myself, and seeing how far short I fall from his beingness. That tends toward self-condemnation. "Hello, my name is Ralph; king Ralphie, I'm being a sludge-bunny". But if I look at, or from, his end of the gap I see possibility. Great possibility. Huge possibility; beyond imagination. We have a saying: "the sky's the limit" (but that was before the space age). But now other realms are opening up: There is no limit. Unseen realms beyond our experience in this physical realm are opening. (Realms in which we have always had existence anyway.) There is no limit; it's way, *way*, WAY beyond the sky! I'm just a baby in it; John is all grown up. (Jesus was all grown up; John is all grown up…commissioned to take us to the next step.) What great good fortune is mine…to have found one who is all grown up!

Back in 2005 when I looked in the mirror into my own eyes and clearly saw that I am Elohim, although I tried to deny it (and couldn't) I still clearly KNOW that I am. (And John explains that deep, deep, deep inside we all know that we are.)

At the present time this is how I assess me. I was born, just as Jesus said, as a pure, innocent, little spark of Life, or the Source, or Meaning, or God --- however I want to think of it (just as I saw it when I first met the Light…and didn't understand). I was Meaning aware. I had just been given a body which I didn't understand, or even know how to use, to be in. Something brand new. My opportunity, being given life in this realm, is to make manifest in form this spark of Life, Meaning, that I am. I have a being: Real me (Meaning aware) has a being (unseen) --- the first level of form. I have a heart, the next level of form. I've spent most of my years developing the next level of form, a "myself", which has been how I've identified me inside --- a more shallow level of form. I've developed a personality, which is how I present me to the world --- an even shallower level of form. All this the world recognizes as my person. I've been living kind of like an iceberg. An iceberg floats with about 3 percent of its mass showing above the waves. About 97 percent is hidden. That's me in myself --- 97 percent hidden. All the Meaning is hidden. I've even carefully, cunningly hidden real me from myself (buried it deep in my subconscious out of sight). I know: I can respond as much as I want to in my heart. I can relax. I can open. I can soften. (Relaxing, opening, softening is not something I do in my conscious mind --- it is something real me does at a level deeper than my conscious mind.)

CHAPTER 5

BACK TO THE 'SPACE RACE'

Jumping around again…

TIMES PAST

I worked for Convair Astronautics for several more years after my initial lay-off in late '67. I worked as a contractor rather than an employee. That meant no company benefits and no unemployment insurance. I worked there most of '69 and then '77 through '79, as I recall (with old guys the memory of some things gets a little fuzzy). I was working there in '69, when the Astronaut Neil Armstrong stepped down onto the surface of the Moon. That was an event watched by hundreds of millions all around the world. What he said: "That's one small step for man, one giant leap for Mankind" is widely quoted and widely remembered. Another quote, not so widely remembered, was voiced by the U S President, Richard Nixon. He said (and I might not be quoting exactly): "For a few moments in time all the peoples of the world were one." The Nixon quote was, perhaps, the more profound in the Big Picture of Mankind.

He probably didn't realise how close his words were aligned with what Jesus said.

Speaking of REAL big steps, I walked later with an Apostle, John Robert Stevens, in a church called "The Walk", and he said, "You've made a big step in going from the Church Age into the Walk. The step from the Walk into the Kingdom is bigger." That was exciting and good food to the ears of a hungry soul looking for more. To me. (I'll explain this later, see Chapter 7,)

PRESENT TIME

I can see that the step John de Ruiter is inviting us to take is really big. I did not, at that time, imagine that it would lead to a change of the Age. Is this the bigger step that John Stevens was seeing?

PHILOSOPHICAL COMMENT

Change to what? New Age? Age of Aquarius? The Kingdom of God? End of Kali Yuga? Kingdom of Heaven? Nirvana? Valhalla? The Happy Hunting Ground? There are SO many stories. Do I need to know what? Isn't moving into something new enough? It's exciting. A change is coming; how fast it comes we can't see yet.

CHAPTER 6

CURIOSITY

I warned that I might jump around, time-wise, with my stories.

TIMES PAST

The conflict between creation and evolution seemed to be raging in some church circles. It seemed to me that both sides were trying to use the information available to prove that God is real, or that there is no God. It seemed to me that I was in a place to look impartially at the information available: I had met God, so I would not be trying to prove anything by what I found in my search. I read many books and articles on both sides of the controversy. I took all the courses in Anthropology offered by the local Community College, plus several courses by correspondence from U C Berkeley. Later this proved useful, or perhaps it turned out to be a big fat rabbit trail.

PHILOSOPHICAL COMMENT

With regard to the conflict between creation and evolution, I had a few thoughts about the creation story in the Book of

Genesis. It says that God created everything in six days. Evolutionists say it took about four billion years. What if the ancient word which was interpreted as "day" was not exactly that. We quickly decide that it meant a 24-hour-day as we know it. What if it were interpreted as a "type-of-day"? What if the first day of creation actually said the first "type-of-day", and it happened to be way over a billion years of our type of day? What if the second "type-of-day" was much shorter, and took only 500,000,000 of our years? And so on, and so on. Then perhaps all of the current conflict and controversy ensued because of a misinterpreted word in an ancient story. Could that be? (Of course, this line of thinking tends to break down as we follow the Genesis story into the sixth and seventh days.) But if we're understanding only about five percent of our universe, could it be something like that? Anyway, should we spend any time worrying about it? If we're using less than 5% of our brains?

TIMES PAST

Again, I warned that I might jump around in time. About three months after I had that spectacular awakening in 1966 I was going to bed early with a headache. It was caused by nervous tension from smoking---nicotine is a nerve poison. I knew how to get rid of it: Lay off smoking for about two days. But I wouldn't. Over a ten-year period, I had tried every method I had ever heard of to quit. My wife said, "You believe in God; ask Him to help you quit." My reaction (in thought only) was: 'No way am I going to make one more old college try to quit, and ask God to shore up my efforts!' I thought that over for three or four days and, when I was going to bed early again with a headache, I earnestly prayed, "God, You make me quit---and I won't help You. I've tried for years, and only proved that I'm a failure. Unable. You make me quit, and I won't help You!" I won't try to help You, try to shore up my efforts to quit again! That was the last cigarette I smoked for 16 years. I couldn't. About three days later, when withdrawal symptoms were at their peak, a friend would stop by my desk at work with a cigarette half-way out of the pack, offering. I couldn't take it from his hand. So, I didn't smoke for 16 years. It was just not a part of my life. We're afraid to believe; to REALLY believe; afraid it would be too wonderful. Then, much later, in 1981, a co-worker became a daddy---and passed out cigars and chocolates. I thought, 'I'm a non-smoker; I can be bold; I can be carefree; I can take a cigar, no problem.' I got hooked on one cigar.

PRESENT TIME

Why, oh why didn't I take the chocolate instead!? That one little chocolate might have saved me from burning up over 30,000 dollars worth of tobacco since then. I know I'll quit for good when I die. I can imagine me on my death bed pleading with the nurse, please, can't you light one up and give me a few drags before I go?

PHILOSOPHICAL COMMENT

When I prayed to God, what was I doing? If Reality (Meaning, God) is different --- and vastly greater --- than my old concept of God, what was I accessing? Real me? Real us? John? What? Could it be that we *really are* all Elohim? Just as Jesus said? If God is not a single separate entity up there somewhere, what is it that I prayed to? I got answers, so it works. I actually saw results. I've received healings and I've healed others. Did I somehow access Real Power, and then just use it for my own purpose in my separation? I got answers. A great many people get answers. What are we doing? With all that Real Power available, what *could* we be doing? And why? Is an answer to prayer received as an invitation to go much deeper? Or does it just bolster a belief that living away from HOME is working out?

TROUBLE

TIMES PAST

My wife and I were having difficulties. We went for counselling to a Spirit-filled Lutheran Pastor (1970) who had been a speaker at that charismatic group which I was attending. The Pastor said, "I can't give you a word from God, but I know a man who can." He suggested we see John Robert Stevens in Los Angeles. He was called an Apostle. We went to see him in a church service in December 1970. I could see, in that one service, that Stevens had more; more of what I had been seeing in reading the Bible. He had more of what I was searching for. I felt like I had come home. We went up to him for personal ministry at the end of the meeting. He said to me, "You've been here before." I answered, "No." He said. "You've been here in spirit." Half a dozen of his Elders nodded affirmative. The result of that trip was that I attended more meetings and got involved with "The Walk" churches. My wife said, "It's wrong."

John Robert Stevens had been kicked out of his church because what he was trying to tell the church leaders was too far out. So, he started his own church. (That appears to have been the procedure followed throughout the history of the expansion of the Protestant Church Movement. One member gets a deeper revelation---it's too much---they kick him out---he starts a new Denomination.) The church which John Robert Stevens started, the Church of the Living Word (known as "The Walk"), was like that. It was a significant cut above the local churches. It was denounced by many. Stevens was referred to as a cult leader. Within the Walk he was known as the Apostle.

This is a bit of the background of John Robert Stevens. Some of this I've heard; some I read in a Doctoral Dissertation on the subject; but that was about 30 years ago, and my memory....? Well, I've already said a bit about my memory. (Can I claim a "senior moment"?) In 1947 a group was praying in a barn at North Battleford, Saskatchewan, Canada. The Holy Spirit came upon them and flames appeared over them—even over the barn. The flames were so apparent that the Fire Department responded. There were obvious flames, but no fire. Later the leaders of that group were travelling around, laying hands on people and blessing them. In 1951 Stevens, who was a Pastor in a church, went to them for ministry in Tacoma, Washington State. The heavens were opened to him. He tried to tell all this to his church back home. They kicked him out. He started his own church.

TIMES PAST

When I first went to a church in "The Walk" I felt like I came home, (Much later, after I met John de Ruiter, I could see that it was just a step in the direction of HOME). It was a significant step, but just a step. There's more. There's always more. We're afraid to believe; afraid it would be too wonderful.

A hallmark of the churches in "The Walk" was singing in tongues; free worshipping in the Spirit. (This manifestation had first appeared earlier, in Edmonton, Alberta.) Picture 600 people, all freely singing in tongues, while the organist played freely in the Spirit. That was more beautiful than any concert by a full symphony orchestra. It was known as "the Song of the Lord." John Robert Stevens was called "the Apostle". He had a lot more of God than anyone else I had met up to that time. He was speaking, teaching and imparting much of what I had glimpsed in studying the Bible.

PHILOSOPHICAL COMMENT

What is an Apostle? In religious systems we were taught to exalt Apostles and Prophets; to build statues and monuments to exalt them. From a Biblical point of view the picture is quite different. The Apostle Paul wrote, "For I think that God has exhibited us apostles as last of all, like men sentenced to death; because we have become a spectacle to the world, to angels and to men. We are fools for Christ's sake, but you are wise in Christ. We are weak, but you are strong. You are held in honor, but we in disrepute. To the present hour we hunger and thirst, we are ill-clad and buffeted and homeless, and we labor, working with our own hands. When reviled, we bless; when persecuted, we endure; when slandered, we try to conciliate; we have become, and are now, as the refuse of the world, the offscouring of all things." First Corinthians 4:9-13, Revised Standard Version. (Ref. 5). In Biblical times it seems that the definition of apostle was one who had been with the Lord. In modern day it seems to be more like one who can be, or is being, with the Lord. Wouldn't that be surrendered enough to be with the Lord? Why do we create the pedestals? What's wrong with this picture? Why does it seem to be upside down?

Someone asked John Stevens why he didn't heal people, because great healing ministries were prominent and had been prominent for a long time. He said that he was interested in healing at a deeper level than just the physical; healing us in spirit.

A number of times I attended meetings in Los Angeles conducted by a famous healing minister. After each meeting truckloads of wheelchairs, crutches and canes would be hauled away from the auditorium. I had already experienced the Baptism in the Holy Spirit, speaking in tongues and being healed several times before I went to those meetings. I attended one such meeting (I was already walking with the apostle John Robert Stevens) and the minister invited all men in the audience who were pastors or elders or some kind of spiritual leaders to come up onto the stage. I went. There were about thirty-five men lined up in a couple of rows on the stage. The minister went down the rows, touching each man on the forehead. Each man touched fell flat on his back (of course two men were working with her to catch each man as he fell). As she approached me I really wanted to let go and see how this felt. She touched me; nothing happened. Thirty-five men lay flat on their backs. I was the only one standing. Only the minister, the two men who caught falling men, and I were standing. It was a spectacle. I wasn't embarrassed; it just was what it was. Curious. They all got up, we all went back to our seats, the minister soared on.

PRESENT TIME

Much later, someone asked John de Ruiter the same question: Why didn't he heal people? He is only interested in calling, or inviting, us to return HOME: to be aware of our actual existence at a deeper level --- at a level that doesn't even relate to physical healing. Healing just the physical is nice, but does it have any profound meaning? I had been healed several times, and I had healed others; did it really invite me/us deeper?

PHILOSOPHICAL COMMENT

Does healing on the surface only cover the infection? Is it like putting salve on a cancer sore? Is the infection that we've left Home? I've always made my life all about myself; is that the infection? If I get a healing of something wrong with my physical body, does that only encourage me to believe that my life away from Home is working? Have I thus stepped aside from another opportunity to realise a little of the Truth? Did I use it as a distraction? Did I just learn how to use a little bit of Real Power available, for my own personal satisfaction? Might I have received it as an invitation to seek more of the Truth? Of Reality?

Do healers and miracle workers just serve as their levels of invitation toward more? Were they fulfilling a level of movement as the veils had been lifted just a little? Were they moving in the small amount of Light afforded at the time? Or were they usurping a little of the Real Power available for their personal reputation? What if instead of just trying to feel better I realize an invitation to be better in whatever I feel? What if my main focus is that I like what I know deep inside and that doesn't need to change how I feel?

TIMES PAST

I was involved in "The Walk" for about 15 years, and have maintained some contact. I had a lot of experiences. Before long I was ordained as an Elder (the same level of authority as a Pastor, but without license to conduct marriages and funerals). Here are some of those experiences; they may be shuffled in time, but I already warned that old guys are apt to get stories shuffled.

CHAPTER 8

"THE WALK"

TIMES PAST

In my initial awakening glimpse, the overpowering experience was of love. Love way beyond my ability to measure, comprehend or contain. Love beyond love. It was too much. But a residue remains; I can't give it all away. I was used to sensing love primarily as an emotion. I could feel love. I could let it flow, or put a damper on it. My normal tendency was to let it flow only to the edge of my comfort zone, and no farther.

PHILOSOPHICAL COMMENT

I find love everywhere: Eye contact in a momentary connection with someone I pass on the street; with a person at the checkout stand; in a hallway; on an elevator; saying "Hi" to a friend. It's often easiest with babies. A quick glance; we drop our guards and it flows. We love. We love that. For a moment we drop back into Reality, into what we really are, into a touch of meeting. Deep, deep inside we know we are all connected. (Of course, the edges of our comfort zones are quickly reached, so we shut it down; but

Goodness already flowed.) Openness of heart, softness of heart, kindness, acceptance of things just as they are is key to returning Home. I finally realized that loving someone is fine. The Source of Life moves as love, so it's natural. The problem starts with the concept "mine"; with the idea of possession. I learned that the thought of possession is normal for me, being self-oriented and away from Home. Trying to tap into a pure flow of goodness, and then wanting to get some personal benefit out of it, throws a monkey wrench into the works. Messes it up. A woman would respond a little more than most and I'd get the idea, 'she's mine.' Wanting to take it for my own benefit, wanting to make it 'mine' can ruin a good and meaningful relationship. MEANING moves as love, therefore it is not an experience first. It is first a movement of Beingness, so it precedes experience. Love is more radical than we can conceive.

TIMES PAST

In "The Walk" churches, under John Stevens, we practised the "laying-on-of-hands" to impart a blessing to someone who asked. I had many experiences when two or three or four of us who were Elders would be laying hands on one person who came for a blessing. I would be just loving the person; just letting the love flow. Sometimes the person would be aware of the flow and aware of where it was coming from, and afterward turn and hug me in thanks. It wasn't me; I was just letting IT flow. I often ministered with one particular Elder for about an hour after a meeting (many meetings). A bunch of people would be lining up. At the end he would be drained, worn out. I would be charged, because by LETTING the love flow I could not give it all away. So, I would bless him (the other Elder), to pick him back up, and then, late at night, still charged, I would drive home a hundred miles. I could see that he was giving more of himself, rather than letting It flow, and that's why he got worn out. Most people who came for a blessing were open to receive. But not all. I remember one young woman who came; three or four of us placed our hands on her head. I was just loving her; I could feel the flow of Presence through my hands, but it wasn't going beyond the surfaces of the palms of my hands. But I still loved her. At the end she turned to me, very angry, and said, "Well! You don't have to drill a hole in my head!" That's what she felt. How did I impart? How does the flow of Presence flow through me?

PHILOSOPHICAL COMMENT

We impart what we are being inside. We react according to what walls and defences we've put in place to protect what we are being. The laying-on-of-hands is especially effective: one is open to receive; one is open to impart. When we pray, when we heal, what are we accessing? There's definitely power at work: What are we doing? Do I learn to use the power, and then usurp some of it for my personal benefit and satisfaction? Is there some level of presumption in the giver? Or in the receiver? Are both using it? Do I use it for affirmation that my "story" away from Home is working? Presumption might be kind of like dropping a pinch of arsenic into the soup.

CHAPTER 9

WANDERING, WONDERING

TIMES PAST

I was visiting friends in Anaheim, California. Six or eight of us were sitting in the living room talking. A low window was open so the cat could come and go freely. The cat came charging through the window and flopped on the floor. It lay there "kicking its last". It was foaming at the mouth and the smell of poison was strong in the room. The cat was dead. (I was raised on a farm where we provided all of our own meat, so I'd seen lots of animals and chickens "kick their last" after they'd been killed.) My conclusion: The cat is dead. Someone suggested that we pray for the cat, and they all gathered around extending their hands over the cat. I didn't have high regard for cats, and I had already concluded that the cat was dead, but I thought I might as well join them. As I did so I felt the strongest flow of the Presence through my hands that I have ever felt. After a minute or two the cat stopped kicking and twitching and got on its belly. Then it stood on its feet. Someone got a saucer of milk and the cat was lapping it up. Someone was wiping up the poison and slobber from the floor. I was a little surprised: Five minutes ago, the cat was dead, now it's lapping up milk. I can't take credit; six or eight of us were praying and extending our hands over the cat. But I was aware of the strongest flow of Presence through my hands that I have ever felt. I have felt the flow a thousand times; but that was the strongest. We're afraid to believe; afraid it would be too wonderful.

PHILOSOPHICAL COMMENT

When we pray, what power are we accessing? What are we reaching into? What are we doing in Reality?

TIMES PAST

I had a lot of dreams about flying—personally (late '60's through middle '80's). I could soar at will all by myself. When the movie "Superman" came out I went back to see it the second time—just for the joy of the scene where Superman took Lois Lane for a flight over the city. I could relate. It was so delicious.

Perhaps the most interesting flying dream I had was this (it was long and intricate; it would have made a good TV program): I was riding in a convertible car with four friends along a narrow winding road on the side of a mountain. Rock cliffs were straight up and straight down on either side of the road. We had the top folded down and three of us were in the back seat with our feet on the seat and sitting on the folded-down top. The driver missed a sharp curve and we sailed off into the air. Somehow the car landed on a steep slope, with lots of brush...we survived.

The time frame shifted a week or so later. In the next scene of the dream the same five of us were on the same road in the same car....and the driver missed the same curve. We knew that survival was possible, and, without talking, we acted together to influence the trajectory of the car. We thought we could "put English" on the car. (When you're playing pool, if you hit the cue ball just a little off center with the cue stick, you can impart a spin to the cue ball, which will transfer a spin to the target ball and affect the outcome. It's called "putting English" on it.) We collectively thought that maybe we could "put English" on the car. It worked. We caused the car to fly. We had survival. In the dream, in the weeks and months ahead we would go up on the high cliffs on weekends and just fly around for fun. We invited close friends and taught them to fly, too. One time we had a test: There was a large piano sitting on a ledge on the side of the cliff, and we were required to move it up onto the road above. Two of us picked it up and easily flew it up onto the road. After that test we flew around with great confidence. We could fly anywhere, do anything. Sometime later three of us flew down to the valley below and landed in a park, with a wide field of grass and large trees around it. There was crowd of about a hundred people off in the distance, and some of them had seen us land. They started walking toward us: 'Who could believe that men could fly and land like that?!' We started walking away. They started running toward us. We began running, fearing the crowd. They were running faster. We ran faster, and we were trying to lift off, to fly away and escape. But we couldn't lift off. They didn't believe that men could fly. We were bogged down in their unbelief. I woke up realizing that we (I) were (was) trapped by the unbelief of the crowd.

We're afraid to believe; to REALLY believe. Afraid it would be too wonderful.

PHILOSOPHICAL COMMENT

I'm not suggesting that I might be able to fly physically, but what if I let my awareness open to other realms (which we belong in anyway)? "Flying" is a good word to describe some of that. Or perhaps dancing in 3-D in multiple levels. Or watching John lead someone into experiencing and realizing being in a deeper realm. That's joy!

In 1971, with the ups-and-downs of the Aerospace Industry, I was down. There was Government money available to re-train some laid-off Aerospace Engineers. I took an intensive course in Pollution Management: Problems with air, water, noise and solid waste pollution. Later (most of 1975) I worked as an Air Pollution Control Engineer for a California county. It was in the low inland desert, an intense agriculture area. Most of the valley is 100 to 200 feet below sea level. It is irrigated from the Colorado River and the run-off goes into the Salton Sea, 250 feet below sea level. In addition to agriculture, there were also a lot of manufacturing and processing facilities which we had to inspect: A sugar beet factory, a cotton-seed oil extraction facility, a drywall manufacturing plant, a fertilizer plant processing dead animal carcasses, several alfalfa pelletizing plants, etc. Everywhere there were vast fields of crops. In one area there were large fields of onions. Industrious honey bees, by the hundreds of thousands, were busily harvesting nectar from the beautiful blue flowers. I thought, 'there must be onion honey somewhere on grocery shelves.' I kept my eye out for the labels on honey jars around Southern California for some time. I found wild flower honey, clover honey, sage honey, alfalfa honey, etc. I never could find jars labelled 'onion honey'.

PHILOSOPHICAL COMMENT

Is there some alternate, more romantic-sounding name for
onions?

TIMES PAST

Once three of us spent a 13-hour day collecting smoke
samples from a factory smoke stack. The air temperature
was 117 degrees Fahrenheit, plus we were working on a roof
in the sun with an occasional swirl of smoke around us. That
was a rough day. The next day was beautiful: I got up early
to catch a little chartered plane to deliver the stack samples
to a laboratory near San Francisco. There were a few big
thunder-heads developing over the San Juaquin valley that
day, so we meandered around them. It was a beautiful trip
that made up for the day before.

While I was working in the low inland desert I got qualified
for a life-time Instructor's Certificate for California
Community Colleges, and taught a night course in Air
Pollution. Much later I taught mathematics to a Grade 9
class for a semester.

In my weekly routine I would jump in my truck at 5 pm
Friday and head for the Coast (because the thermometer
reached 115 degrees F. every day in the desert). I would

attend a couple meetings at "Walk" churches during the weekend, and drive back to the desert early Monday morning.

> *"And a highway shall be there,*
> *and it shall be called the Holy Way;*
> *the unclean shall not pass over it,*
> *and fools shall not err therein."*
>
> Isa 35:8 RSV (Ref. 5)

I dreamed (early 1970s) that a few of us friends were gathering for a meeting in a little clearing in the country. It was night, and VERY dark. As we waited for the meeting time people were milling around, visiting in groups of two or three, chatting about light every-day things. Each person had two eyes that looked like little flashlights: The beams of light were narrow cones and not very bright. The beams extended only about 15 feet (5 meters), and a person could see only what was illuminated by his/her two little flashlight-beam eyes. It was VERY dark. I felt an urge to back away a bit to get a bigger overall view. As I did I backed up a small rise, and the earliest light of morning began to make the landscape visible. The little clearing was in very rough country: Steep gullies, sharp hills, rocks everywhere from basketball-size to house-size. And everything was overgrown with trees and brush so thick you couldn't walk through. As the pre-dawn got lighter I could see that the little clearing where we were gathering was actually in the middle of a graded road-bed. The road-bed was perfectly formed, and perfectly graded, but never paved. It had been there for a long time, because small bushes and grass and native plants had overgrown it---so extensively that it was camouflaged. You could be right in the middle of it and not recognize that it was a road. It was wide---wide enough for six or eight lanes of freeway. It was smooth---it contained no dips nor rises. It was straight as an arrow, climbing gently through the rough foothills toward the mountain horizon to the east. And although it went through VERY rough, rocky country, not one rock nor one tree protruded into the edge of the road (not even into the graded ditch drop-offs on each side). As the dream ended, the sun was about to pop up. And it would rise exactly where the highway went over the horizon.

PHILOSOPHICAL COMMENT

What I understood from the dream was that we were in a time of great darkness. We couldn't see. We had very protracted vision. But the roadway was already prepared; it had been laid out and established a long time ago. The sun comes up at the appointed time. Although we strive to see more, our striving cannot hurry it's rising. A change is coming; how fast it comes we can't see yet.

PRESENT TIME

Years later, when John de Ruiter talked about a pilot hole being formed, and it being expanded into a highway, and he talked about *us* becoming a highway upon which many could easily walk, I recalled that dream with a deeper level of understanding.

PHILOSOPHICAL COMMENT

The dawning of something new is coming. As more light is given it will be possible to see the way. In the fullness of the Light the way will be a highway for many to walk thereon. We walk in the light we have available. If we can see only 15 feet by the light of two dim, narrow-beam flashlights, we walk our best in that; until more light is available. We walk anticipating more light. Something new is coming. We don't create it --- it's been laid out of ancient times. I *could* choose to be a tiny part. There's always more. We're afraid to believe; afraid it would be too wonderful.

TIMES PAST

Another time I had a very small vision. I was visiting a "Walk" church in Grand Junction, Colorado in '75 or '76. We were in a time of free worship in the Spirit. I saw the very beginning of the approaching dawn in an almost clear sky. Little clouds from all over the sky rushed to the East and clumped together and blanketed the eastern sky and horizon. They made it appear as if the dawn was not coming; that darkness still prevailed. But I KNEW that you can't hold back the dawn. At the right time the sun comes up, and the whole landscape is illuminated, clouds or no clouds. Something new is coming. The world of today, and the regimes that govern, may try to hide Reality; but they are "little clouds" as compared to the sunrise.

PHILOSOPHICAL COMMENT

What did I realize? A change is coming; the dawning of something new; and nothing can stop it. We don't set the timing; it's already set. Our efforts cannot cover it over, nor hide it, nor slow it down. We (earth dwellers) don't initiate profound events; not anymore than we can initiate the time of the sunrise. When the fullness of the time arrives, it happens. In many church circles there is a widespread, growing realization that veils are being removed, that seeing is increasing, because of the timing. (Ref.4.)

CHAPTER 10

GO NORTH, YOUNG MAN, GO NORTH

TIMES PAST

In 1974 I started getting the idea that God was telling me to move back to Alberta, Canada. 'No, God, no! Not Alberta!' I remembered too many times freezing my hands and feet growing up working on the homestead. Living for years in the San Diego area had spoiled me. We had a 5-bedroom, 3-bath house on a ridge with a 270-degree view: Mt Palomar to the northeast, six ranges of the Laguna Mountains to the east, and a lake far below us to the west. Every couple of years it would snow on Mt. Palomar; we could see it from our living room. We would pack up the family and drive up to play in the snow. When we got cold we would drive back down to the orange groves. Leave that to go to Alberta?! So, I was seriously seeking confirmation that it was direction from God. I didn't want such a huge decision to be based on some hair-brained idea generated in my own head. After five years, in late 1979, I had gotten enough confirmation (from multiple sources, some with no involvement whatsoever) that I decided to move. By then the kids were grown and had moved away. Our marriage had dwindled away to zero over a 10-year period, and we divorced. (I think working with the idea of moving to Canada had been one contributing factor in the dwindling.) I moved in 1980. It cost me my marriage, my family, my job, my career, all my money, my good credit rating, the opinions of my friends and relatives and my Country. After I moved I had to wait 16 years to find out why; to meet John de Ruiter. In all that time I never had doubts about the profound wisdom of the move; I always KNEW that Alberta was the place for me to be. I was always secure in some kind of knowing inside that I was led here by God; or I was following the Source; or responding to a calling; or?? I have modified some of my vocabulary; I might think of reality in different terms than I used to; but the direction has always been the same. This is where, after the 16 years, I would meet John de Ruiter and change everything. What did Mark Twain say? 'The two best days of your life: The day you were born and the day you found out why.'

CHAPTER 11

SCHOOLBOY AGAIN

TIMES PAST

In '75 – '76 I went back to school for a Master's degree. I had nine months remaining of GI Bill money for schooling, and it was about to expire. I had determined that I could earn a Master's Degree in Civil Engineering in that time at the University of Utah, so I moved to Salt Lake City. There was a strong "Walk" church there. University was going fine; I made good grades except for one course: Soils Engineering. The Professor didn't like me at all. We had some kind of a personality clash, without ever voicing anything. He rode me through the whole course and gave me a grade of D. I couldn't graduate with the class; I had enough credits, but you had to have a Grade Point Average of "B" or better to graduate and that one grade dropped me just below a "B". Government money ran out, (I had used all the educational benefits under the GI Bill), so I got three part-time jobs and signed up for two easy courses for summer school. I got "A's" in both, and quietly received my degree in August. The three part-time jobs I got: One was flipping burgers at a fast-food café; one was driving a University-owned van to carry wheel-chair students to and from classes; and one was working for a temp-labor company, where you'd show up at 6 am and go out to work for whomever called in for temporary laborers that day. The dirtiest job I ever had was "swamper" on a vacuum truck. The truck was a big vacuum cleaner, six feet in diameter by 18 feet long. It was used to suck out such things as car-wash sumps and septic tanks. My job was to put on waterproof clothes, including boots, gloves and cap, get into the truck through a 20-inch man-way in the top, and shovel out the residue in the bottom, which wouldn't flow out through a 12-inch nozzle at the back when the truck was unloaded. Lucky for me, the owner had sucked out a couple of car-wash sumps that morning, instead of septic tanks.

PRESENT TIME

Much later, in the year 2000, I became qualified by Transport Canada as a Highway Tank Engineer, authorized to design such vacuum tanks, or any highway tank for transporting dangerous goods, and large diesel tanks for drilling rigs and work camps anywhere in Canada. I designed quite a few.

CHAPTER 12

COLD WAR JITTERS

TIMES PAST

Much earlier, for some ten years (early 1960's through early 1970's) we, as a family, had been suffering from Cold War jitters, as many, many people did. We worried about survival, food storage, bomb shelters, etc. and considered moving to a quieter part of the Country. Most of our vacations were spent touring the Northwest: Checking out towns, schools, colleges, work, etc. We were searching for a means of support for the family somewhere in the Northwest. I had nine more months of schooling left on the G I Bill (this was way before I used it to get a Master's Degree), and I had enough background in Anthropology to enter a PhD Program at Washington State University. So, I did. I was accepted into a PhD Program in Physical Anthropology. We had been trying to sell our house for a couple of years, and finally it sold. We were free to move to Eastern Washington. I went to John Robert Stevens for ministry, and confirmation from a higher level that this would be a good move. I don't remember the exact words he spoke, but essentially he said, You've made some DUMB decisions in your life, but if you do this, it will be the

DUMBEST! I fully took that in, and in 20 or 30 seconds I changed my mind. What kind of a career could I have in Anthropology, anyway? I could teach Anthropology or excavate old sites; very few other types of jobs would be available in that field. I had already studied as much Anthropology as interested me. My interest level in that field had waned to almost zero. My mind was changed. (I didn't want to talk about the OTHER dumb decisions in my life that John Stevens was referring to.) I went home and said to my wife, "Scratch the move to Washington". My wife was disappointed, vexed: Ten years of reasoning, searching, planning---cancelled. (I suspect that at least one of her motives in the later years of our relationship was to get me moved as far away from the "cult" leader John Robert Stevens as possible.)

CHAPTER 13

THE OUTER PLANETS

TIMES PAST

Here I go again, jumping around with my stories---I warned that old guys' stories get shuffled time-wise. During all of 1977 I was back at Convair Astronautics and I worked on the Voyager Program. Voyager 1 and 2 were launched in August and September of 1977. Their missions: To explore the outer planets (Jupiter, Saturn, Uranus and Neptune) and beyond. This was called "The Grand Tour", and planetary alignment which would allow this occurs only once in 176 years. The next conjunction will be in 2153. (Ref.14). I was working in the Guidance Group. I didn't write the Guidance Equations; the guidance wizards did that. I simulated the trajectories on a main-frame computer from launch to burn-out, and did it about 75 times for each flight. This was so that the guidance wizards could tweak the many little factors in the equations to ensure that at burn-out the spacecraft(s) had a speed and precise direction that would cause them to coast all the way to Jupiter. The task also fell to me to flow-chart the Guidance Equations (about 45 pages of hand-written flow-chart; nearly 500 decision boxes) and publish them in a report: "The Convair Real-Time Guidance System."

I mentioned earlier that we have to reach a speed of 37,000 feet per second (40,600 kilometers per hour (kph)) to go to the Moon. To coast all the way to Jupiter, on a minimum-energy trajectory, we must leave Earth with a speed of about 99,000 kph. (Ref. 3). But it would take years to get there (Ref. 17) ----far too long to accommodate "The Grand Tour". To go on a fast-track trajectory, we needed about 140,000 kph. Voyager 1 departed with a velocity of 143,000 kph; Voyager 2 with 140,000 kph. (Ref. 14). Then the spacecraft(s) did a "crack-the-whip maneuver" around Jupiter to gain enough speed to go to Saturn. V2 approached Jupiter at 46,000 kph; departed at 86,000 kph, in Nov '79. V1 approached Jupiter at 38,000 kph; departed at 75,000 kph, in Mar '79. (Ref. 14). Then the space-crafts did a similar maneuver at Saturn to go on to Uranus, and to Neptune, and on. They are still sending back data, from the edge of the Solar System or beyond (Google JPL Voyager). The last time I googled it (2018) they had been sailing/coasting/falling for over 40 years; Voyager 2 had swept past Jupiter, Saturn, Uranus and Neptune, and escaped our solar system. Voyager 1 is travelling North, more toward the North Star. And, they were still sending back data, from beyond the reaches of our solar system. My signature is on board both spacecrafts: The people involved in the Project signed our names to be photographically printed on six aluminum plates to be put on board. Also, on each craft is a record in 47 Earth languages, introduced by the UN Secretary General, inviting anyone to come visit us on Earth. Maybe some alien will come looking for me some day. (I'm not holding my breath; there are 5400 names on the list.)

That's why I like the movie "Starman". It starts off with the launch of Voyager; then some alien traveller finds it, removes the record inviting him to visit Earth. He comes. As soon as he enters our atmosphere we track him and, of course, we shoot him down. Then the adventure unfolds. The alien replicates the deceased husband of a local woman, kidnaps her and demands to be driven to Arizona.

PHILOSOPHICAL COMMENT

She was kidnapped. However, did we (people) come up with a term like kidnapped in our language? If a child were taken it would make sense. But a grown-up person? And we have another odd term in our language: "Cat nap". Maybe because cats sleep a lot. I once read of a home invader who stole a cat. That would be a cat kidnapped. I guess that if the cat snoozed on the trip that would be a kid-napped cat cat nap. If he had stolen a baby goat, that would be a kid kidnapped. If the baby goat fell asleep on the trip, that would be a kidnapped kid cat nap. Some of the terms in our language are expressive, but funny.

It was interesting being a little part of a team sending spacecrafts to Jupiter and beyond, but there was always something in the back of my mind of the profound level that was more interesting. I was always knowing that there's more. I was always searching for more. When you've seen IT, or ??.... when you've stood in the Presence of something so wonderful!...you have an itch somewhere inside where you can't scratch. That happened to the guy in the movie "Close Encounters of the Third Kind". He had a powerful pull, a drawing inside toward something, and he didn't know what. Something was gnawing at him inside and it drove him a little nuts. I was searching, searching ... something was gnawing at me inside...but I didn't get that crazy. (My wife, however, might have had an alternate opinion.)

CHAPTER 14

GLIMPSES AND DREAMS

TIMES PAST

On one of our family driving vacations (1966 or '67) we drove up to Alberta (from San Diego) and stayed with an old neighbor, who had purchased the old homestead. I got up early and walked back up to the old house where I was born and raised. I stood in the yard: The sky was blue, there was no breeze, and it was quiet. It was SO quiet! Not even a bird chirped. It was awesome quiet! I felt a deep peace; a very deep peace inside. It was a profound experience. Much, much later I realized that that was just one of the many little invitations to come back HOME: To Real HOME.

I had a little dream (sometime in '79). I was walking down the sidewalk in Spirit River, Alberta (the town listed on my Birth Certificate). I had only the coat on my back and a little cassette tape player in my hand. (I was listening to a lot of taped messages by John Robert Stevens during that time, so the tape recorder meant "The Word" to me.) As I walked down the sidewalk, in my dream, I didn't know where I would sleep, or eat. It was getting dark; and it was starting to snow. I felt completely at peace in my heart, because I

KNEW that God had sent me there. I understood that to be one of the many confirmations of my planned move back to Alberta. Much later I also realized that it was one more invitation to return HOME: To Real HOME.

PRESENT TIME

I was taking a trip north and we were driving down the street in Spirit River and I was recounting that dream. I couldn't finish it without crying. I guess this experience was reinforcing the message that it brought the first time. John de Ruiter explains that an experience or a dream is like a messenger bringing a message. I tend to look at the messenger (the experience) and sort of skip the message. I *could* get more quiet inside and explore the message.

MOVING NORTH

TIMES PAST

In August 1980, I got the best job offer I had ever received. It
was working for a large Aerospace Company at the Western
Test Range about 120 miles northwest of Los Angeles, on the
coast. I had been there several times. It was a quiet, beautiful
place to live, and with very good money. But I had decided,
and it was confirmed, that I was moving back to Alberta---I
was just waiting for the paperwork to come through. It
wouldn't be fair to the Company to accept the job---but I was
broke! ---and then quit a couple of months later. I turned the
job offer down. About six weeks later the paperwork from
Canada came through: I was licensed to practice Engineering
in Alberta, and/or permitted to immigrate. I immigrated.

There was a strong "Walk" church in Edmonton, so that
made the move easier. I was broke and out of work and a
family took me in. I moved in November 1980. It was getting
kind of late in the Fall to be moving North, but I had been in
Edmonton a year earlier in late November, starting the
paperwork for the move: Then there was no snow and the
weather was nice. But in 1980 when I crossed the border into

Alberta it started to snow. I guess Old Man Winter was welcoming a San Diego man to Alberta. (I used to say "Old Man Winter", but since I've gotten so old, now I say "Mister Winter".)

A little later we built a new church/school building on an acreage near Edmonton. I did the design work, prepared the drawings, obtained building permits, and acted as project Engineer throughout the building and final inspection of the project.

In Edmonton I looked for work, but couldn't find any. I was a registered Professional Engineer; I had a Bachelor's Degree and a Master's Degree and a lot of pretty high-tech experience on my resume. Everywhere I applied for work the answer was, 'we don't need a man so heavily qualified'. So, after a few months I was working for a casual labor supply company: Every morning you'd show up at 6 am, and go to work for whomever called for day-laborers that morning. Then one day I saw l little ad for a draftsman/estimator in the paper. I went. I answered only the questions on his application form. I did not give him my high-sounding resume. I did not tell him I was an Engineer. He hired me on the spot. About a year later he needed an Engineer on his payroll in order to upgrade his Quality Control Program to an International level. I said," Well, I'm an Engineer." (If I had told him that at first he would not have hired me.) The result: I became Chief Engineer and Quality Control Manager for an aggressive company (a welding shop) that grew to 150 employees, doing $25 million in business every year. It was a high-stress, responsible position, because all technical and quality control problems had to be resolved at my desk. I worked well under pressure. And I found it satisfying: Receiving requirements for equipment, sizing and designing the equipment, sourcing materials (because everything we built had to be bid on fixed-price contracts), instructing the Drafting Department on what drawings were required, advising the Purchasing Agent what to buy, obtaining registrations and permits-to-build from the Provincial Authority, watching the equipment being built in the shop (keeping tabs on detailed quality control issues), and watching the equipment depart by truck. It was a satisfying career.

The boss and I developed a good working relationship: Many a Friday evening the shop would shut down at 5 pm and everyone would leave. I would go into the boss's office; he would pull a bottle of whiskey (his favorite) from his desk drawer and a bottle of vodka (my favorite) and we would spend some time solving many of the problems at the local, Municipal, Provincial and Federal levels. Sometimes we even addressed a few International problems. We seldom talked about work because it was after hours. The boss was nearly bald. What little hair still grew he kept shaved off. A couple times I heard him quote that old saying: "God made a few good heads; the rest He covered with hair."

PHILOSOPHICAL COMMENT

Jesus told his disciples, "Peace I leave with you; My peace I give you: not as the world gives, do I give to you. Let not your hearts be troubled, neither let them be afraid." Jn 14:27 RSV (Ref 5) Having at least a small revelation of that was often a calming factor in a busy welding shop. When mistakes were made (not infrequent) many, including some foremen and the boss, first thought "Who screwed up? Who's to blame?" As Chief Engineer and Quality Control Manager the ball soon landed in my court. It seemed that my first thought was always "How can we fix the problem in the fastest, most inexpensive manner to produce a product built to Code with paperwork to prove that it met the Quality Control Program?" The boss paid the bills; did the hiring and firing. The shop foreman tried to meet schedule. For engineering and quality control the buck stopped at my desk. "...My peace I give to you; not as the world gives..." It always seems we are seeking the peace-of-the-world, or the peace that the world gives: The absence of conflict and stress. Peace on that level is often nowhere to be found. The peace in me often influenced the outcome and speeded things along.

TIMES PAST

When quitting time came, if the workload would allow, I would switch off the light, switch off my mind and walk away. There might be four or five jobs spread out on my desk, with the highest priority on the top of the pile. I would leave the desk in a condition which most described as "a mess". But in the morning when I switched on the light, and switched on my mind, I was back in full swing in twenty seconds.

PHILOSOPHICAL COMMENT

Edmonton is a widely spread-out northern city. The population of the greater Edmonton area is close to a million. It's called the "Gateway to the North." There are many manufacturing companies and many service companies here, because we supply activities (including much mining, drilling and exploration) for 3000 miles northward. Edmonton is about 2000 miles north of the Mexican border and 2000 miles south of the Arctic Ocean. The road to Mexico is almost all freeway with no traffic lights. All-weather roads connect Edmonton with Yellowknife and Inuvik in the Northwest Territories, with

Whitehorse and Dawson City in the Yukon, and with Anchorage, Fairbanks and Prudhoe Bay in Alaska. The climate around Edmonton is.......well, variable. Someone described our four seasons as: Almost Winter (Autumn); Winter; Almost Not Winter (Spring); and Road Repair. With the thawing and freezing in the Spring the roads develop a lot of cracks and little holes, called "pot-holes". I heard that the Edmonton Police put on an intensive day to catch impaired drivers (people driving erratically): They stopped six drunks and about 40 pothole dodgers.

When working at the welding shop my normal morning routine was standard: Juice, coffee, cigarette, bacon and eggs, coffee, shift my mental make-up into high gear for all the decisions a Chief Engineer had to make during the day, and head out the door. Just before I left one morning (early '90's) a little bird flew into the patio door, and landed on the back porch upside down. 'Oh, well, it's probably dead, sorry, I'm late, I'll take care of it when I get home (if the neighbor's cat doesn't take care of it).' I went to work. I came home about 9 hours later and noticed that the little bird was still on my back porch upside down. Then I noticed it's feet twitching slightly. I went out and picked it up and cupped it in my hands and spoke softly to it. "You poor little guy. Have you been lying here all day long? You poor little guy!" I closed my hands over it. I felt a flow of Presence through my hands---not strong. After a couple of minutes, I felt it stirring. I opened my hands; it got on its feet; it opened its eyes, and looked around, getting very alert. I imagine it thought 'Oh! My God! I'm sitting on the hand of a people person!' It quickly flew away. I went back into the house, poured a glass of vodka and fixed a steak.

CHAPTER 16

SCHOOLBOY AGAIN AGAIN

TIMES PAST

After I semi-retired ('94) I decided to earn a PhD (Doctor of Philosophy). I didn't bowl, run, skate, ski, snow-board, swim, play bingo, sky-dive---only watch old western movies and drink vodka. I needed something to do. So, I enrolled in a University by correspondence for a PhD in Mechanical Engineering. (Anyway, I always thought it would be fun to write a PhD after my name.) I did all the coursework, established a research project, got approved by a team of advisers, and started research. Then I met John de Ruiter and the project seemed meaningless; so I stopped. John said that I could, I should, come back HOME and work on a real P.H.D. (Post HOME Development). That seemed meaningful. So I joined a large group of perhaps hundreds who have earned an A.B.D. (All But Dissertation). You don't get a certificate for that. My project was a different design for a wind power generator. After I started looking at the design, I didn't think it would be as efficient as the propeller designs that are widely used. But a few years later I saw advertised on TV a smaller version for home use of a very similar design. I don't think it caught on.

CHAPTER 17

MORE GLIMPSES

PRESENT TIME

I was attending a family reunion of many cousins on my mother's side of the family. A cousin had traced the family tree back about 900 years. The reunion was the 100-year anniversary of my grandparents moving to Canada. They were a hardy pioneer family homesteading in north-central Alberta. My cousin had located many current family members, so 81 people, from all over (even from Europe), were attending a dinner in a community hall. A picture of my grandparents, a handsome young couple, hung on the wall. Toward the end of the meal I turned and looked at their picture; and I spontaneously started crying. My sense of it was that I touched them where they are; a connection in a deeper realm. The feeling I experienced was of kindness; their kindness toward all of us gathered. I turned and looked through tearing eyes at all of us in the hall. A sense of kindness pervaded the hall, of us toward them, but very subtle, not nearly as strong as the kindness of them toward us.

PHILOSOPHICAL COMMENT

How free are we to touch other realms? Did I initiate a touch? Or did my cousin, who spent so much time and energy researching the family tree and organizing the reunion, create the possibility of that connection? Or was it initiated from beyond this realm? I think that the Big Picture is a bit bigger that we ever imagined.

John once explained that opening and softening my heart, that letting go of issues and opinions, has an effect (although it may be slight, it may be subtle) both backward and forward down through the generations of my family tree. That's hard to think about with my concept of what time is but, using only about 5% of my brain, is my concept of time really valid? Or, does time pertain only to this physical realm? To this, the most shallow of all the realms in which we exist?

PRESENT TIME

I had a small experience sitting in a dentist chair. Over the years, visiting the dentist has been one of my least-favorite experiences in life. I was getting my teeth cleaned. It hurt. My mouth is very sensitive, and when it come to pain, I'm a wuss. As I lay there hurting, suddenly I was above my body looking down. I could see everything that was happening. I was aware that my body was hurting, but I could not relate to the pain. That lasted throughout the cleaning…about a half hour. That happened only once; the next time I went to the dentist, it hurt.

More recently I dreamed I drowned in a swimming pool and died. A few friends and relatives were mourning my death. I was watching everything. It was not scary nor frightening nor sad. No fear. It was not a very bright nor clear nor pronounced dream; it was just dim and ordinary and quiet and quite okay. I just didn't have a body anymore. I related it to that small wonderful, enlightening, profound experience I had had in the dentist chair having my teeth cleaned, when I was above and watching what the dentist was doing and feeling no pain. When I was orienting me as awareness, or as a more real aspect of me, instead of just being focused on myself. I guess death is just routine…everybody does it.

Looking back, that little experience in the dentist chair was quite profound. This little dream confirmed and crystallized it in place; brought it into realization: Real me is awareness; myself is just the shallow experiences I'm having living in this body. So why have any fear of dying? I was very okay about the whole thing; it was normal, ordinary.

A lot of books have been written by people who temporarily died; I referenced three of them (Ref. 9, 11, and 16). And I've read others over the years. It seems to me that those people just went into awareness, or opened up their awarenesses to more of what they really are (what we all really are). They could see that they weren't gone just because their bodies were not functional. I guess we really don't have to be near death to get real. Perhaps a post-death experience is pretty much the same as a near death experience??? Perhaps my experience was not a N.D.E. (near-death-experience) but rather a N.D.C. (near-dentist's-chair).

PHILOSOPHICAL COMMENT

What did I learn? As real me, by opening up to even some of the realms, such a thing is possible. It is not to be used by myself for pain relief nor for personal comfort. I also learned that I don't need a body to be Real me. I don't need any form to be me. Dozens of glimpses over the years; some big, some small, some tiny, some massive. What would I be if I really, *really* let them all in?

PRESENT TIME

Back in 2005 when I looked at myself in the mirror and clearly saw what I interpreted (according to my learning and training and belief structure) as the eyes of God, I tried to deny it. Why? "That's too big." "How could I be that?" "It would be arrogant to presume that!" "I'm not worthy." "I don't dare to accept that." "I don't dare to say that." "I don't dare to be that." "People will call me crazy." "What could I think that I'm trying to be?"

PHILOSOPHICAL COMMENT

Of course, as myself in myself, all such thoughts, objections, reasoning and arguments are believable. As myself, trying to be that Profound Reality is impossible; absurd. But all such arguments are in myself as elements of my "story." If I'm identified as alone, separate and sovereign, then am I really trying to be the highest authority in my life? Just me myself? King Ralphie? How silly is that? But...if I really let myself return Home, what would the picture look like?

I remember a saying "all dogs go to heaven". Was it a title of a book? A movie? I don't remember (but us old guys have our excuses). "All dogs go to heaven". Is that true for sludge-bunnies? Can we say "all sludge-bunnies go to heaven?" I think the answer is yes. Reading books like Mary Niels and Dr. Alexander and many others, I'd say yes without a doubt; "all sludge-bunnies go to heaven". So, it's probably not a question of going or not going; I'm seeing the opportunity to develop some post-home development

(P.H.D.) before I go, while I'm still living in these dense forms. I see it as just an invitation, an awesome opportunity.

CHAPTER 18

FOUND IT!

Here I go jumping around again --- worse than ever. Chronology is not so important. A mosaic of glimpses and experiences that form a Real picture is vital, precious. Finding IT wasn't easy; the road was fraught with cracks, speed bumps and potholes.

PRESENT TIME

In 1996 I saw a picture of John de Ruiter with his motorcycle in an Edmonton paper. The very short article talked of John as a teacher of a little flock. 'This I've got to check out,' was my response inside (I was always looking for more). I was cautious during the first few meetings which I attended. Suspicious? John Robert Stevens had died in '83 and the Edmonton "Walk" church had disintegrated over the next few years. I had visited quite a few churches and preachers and teachers, searching. That effort was disappointing. I always realized that I already understood more than what they were talking about. The teachers and preachers and leaders of discussion groups which I visited couldn't see as much as I had glimpsed and read about in studying the Bible and walking with John Robert Stevens. So, visiting other churches was kind of like coasting --- with a deep hunger still lingering in my heart. I was looking for more; so I was walking gingerly (suspiciously?). I had been ripped off by "men-of-God" before. Volunteer work and investments had cost me thousands.

TIMES PAST

Just before I left San Diego in '80 John Stevens called a special meeting of the Walk churches in the San Diego area. He spoke a message titled "Give God His Voice." It was verse after verse after verse from the Bible, setting forth a vision that God wants to live in us and manifest through us (as I understood it). After he died in '83, and the Edmonton church fell apart, I lived in that message for about 10 years. In '93—'94 I was beginning to experience the Presence in my body. It was like a sweet, lovely weight in and all through my body. Some mornings I would lie in bed an extra half hour just wallowing in the experience of the Presence before going to work to design oilfield equipment at the welding shop. Then a friend, who had been functioning as an Elder in the past placed his hands on my head to bless me in '94. The result was that I felt like a cement cap was on my head that prevented me from reaching into the delicious touch of the Presence, which I had been enjoying for two or three years. Every time I tried to reach in, to pray, to seek God, all I got was this strong pain on the top of my head. The heavens were brass. That remained for over two years. It was broken a few months after I met John de Ruiter. Being with John that pain gradually receded: It was gone in less than a year.

PHILOSOPHICAL COMMENT

I perceive that we impart what we are being inside. When we speak, when we teach, when we touch, we impart what we are being in the depths of our hearts. Did he impart a cap? Did I want to accept a blockage --- a shield against being Reality? Knowing somewhere deep inside how much that might cost me? What levels of walls have I erected to protect my personal sovereignty? I walk along, my eyes get opened to a little glimpse of where this is going --- what it will cost: I back off for a time --- maybe for a few months, maybe for a few years.

PRESENT TIME

When I attended my first meeting with John de Ruiter I left the meeting early because the pain on the top of my head was so severe. A few months later a friend talked me into going to another meeting. (I think that my friend saved me from the mud puddle in which I was wallowing.) Going to that meeting as I walked across a parking lot toward the meeting place I met John just dismounting from his motorcycle. Our eyes met; we connected. The kindness, the softness, the flow of love… I didn't realise until later that that short connection was the beginning of the end for "myself"; the demise of "my story"; the further awakening of me --- Real me. I finally realized that the view of the way I regarded "myself" was sunk!

By the end of several meetings with John de Ruiter I could see and recognize what he is. I could see what he is being: One with the Presence; the same as the Light; being Reality; opening up and explaining the deepest things that Jesus taught. He was showing me the reality of what I saw in my initial awakening, when I perceived myself as one of the tiny specks of Light. I was still exercising my cautious nature, checking out John against what I knew of the Bible. After several months, however, seeing that John's every response was what I considered perfect, I realized that I was checking out what I knew of the Bible by what John was saying. Mostly it was a good match; in some places I had to stretch my understanding a little bit…in some quite a bit.

PHILOSOPHICAL COMMENT

"The Bible was written for people who are HOME," John said once. To read it only with the understanding of my natural mind (away from HOME) leaves too much room for misinterpretation. The Bible says the same thing: "First of all you must understand this, that no prophecy of scripture is a matter of one's own interpretation, because no prophecy ever came by the impulse of man, but men moved by the Holy Spirit spoke from God." 2 Peter 1:20,21 (Ref.5). There seems to have been a significant number of instances in history wherein someone made a private interpretation of scripture to justify a personal power regime.

TIMES PAST

I was attending a seminar, or retreat, of "Walk" churches in L.A. (in 1982). The retreat had been billed as a music conference, but in meeting after meeting John Stevens was speaking about oneness. At the end of the conference, when we were in a period of free worship (singing in tongues), I silently, fervently, earnestly, desperately prayed," God, when am I going to stand in Your Presence as in that first moment of meeting?" (in 1966). The answer came so swift and so emphatic that I evaluated it as an audible voice that I heard: "Don't come alone!" I could instantly see what that meant. I KNEW what it meant: In the Presence is Oneness. In the Presence separateness and aloneness cannot be. I belong; we belong. That was a glimpse; a significant glimpse; an invitation. I belong. It set a direction---and left a huge mystery. I could spin the wheels of my brain for years trying to contemplate the depth of this mystery. I did. They spun. It took many, many, many years to begin to grasp the full impact of that message: we are One; it is all One.

PRESENT TIME

Much later (about 1999) John de Ruiter was explaining something about Oneness---I don't remember what. Because I was tracking so closely with him, I was watching water slowly collecting on the tip of a leaf. I watched it grow into a drop of water too heavy to hang on. It fell. I was identified as that drop. Falling, falling, falling; I was very okay with being a drop of water and falling. It (I) landed---splash! ---into water (like the ocean). Surprise! Then I could see it (me) submerged in the water, still a drop. I could see the outline of the little sphere that was the drop; like a tiny water-filled balloon submerged in the water. Then the outline started to slowly disappear; starting at one point on the visible circle, it was slowly being erased around the circle. Finally, there was only one little point left that still identified the circle. The point stayed. I was gone. But I wasn't gone. A glimpse of Oneness? An invitation? A mystery. The mystery of Oneness.

I was watching a flock of little birds; there were about a hundred of them. They were flying in perfect formation. The whole flock was sweeping, twisting, turning, diving, climbing, doing barrel rolls----all very fast and in perfect formation. As near as I could tell they were all evenly spaced, close together and moving as a unit. How do they do that? How do they move as one? How does oneness work? Is it possible we could move like that? What if each little bird decided that it wanted or needed to do its own thing? There would be mass confusion. Chaos in the sky. Then, would they look more like all of us? Chaos on the ground?

I went to a hockey game to watch the Edmonton Oilers play. A friend drove so I could comfortably take a drink of vodka before we left. I took a small water bottle, cut half with vodka. In the coliseum, we both bought large glasses of beer, so I was well relaxed watching the game. Suddenly, I was out of the way and John de Ruiter was looking through my eyes. It was very, *very* clear. I (he) looked slowly all around at the crowd in the coliseum as if making invitation: "Come back Home". It was a beautiful and nice and bizarre experience. Later, I confirmed with John that it actually had happened. I can see that it's possible for us to move as one. I *could* let "myself" get out of the way. I *could* identify as real me instead of as "myself". I could *like* being that. How does oneness work? For a very short time, I actually *gave* my space to John, to Reality. When I was visiting Jerusalem, I wanted to see the Golden Gate because the story is that Jesus entered the City through it. He was riding a donkey and his followers were laying down palm branches on the road before him and singing "Hosanna to the Highest". I was impressed to tears. I discussed this with a friend and he suggested, "maybe you were there in a former life?" I said, "No, it's more likely because I'm one with the one who is one with the One who rode the donkey".

PHILOSOPHICAL COMMENT

Is it possible that we could move in Truth as the flock of birds in a similar fashion? That would certainly play havoc with my personal determination of how I walked. How much would I have to give up? What is oneness? When two drops of water meet there is still only one drop of water. When a drop of water falls into the ocean it becomes the ocean. I was discussing this with a friend and he said, "No, it doesn't become the ocean; it's lost; it disappears." I suppose it's how you look at it. From the point of view of me being a separate, sovereign being---I'm lost. If I look at it from the point of view that I belong, that I'm part of it, then I become the ocean. But I don't command the ocean. I'm just not the one in command. What I saw as I was a little drop of water which fell into the ocean was that I was *not* gone---I just wasn't a separate, sovereign drop anymore. All I have to let go of is me myself being in command. Does "myself" *really* want to command the ocean? Or can I be okay rolling with the waves? Even if I crash, deep inside I'm still real me; I can be okay. When the hundred little birds were doing acrobatics in perfect formation, who, or what was in command?

Visions and dreams and awakenings and realizations have to come in some sort of language or pictures which we can relate to in our present level of understanding. If they didn't, we couldn't relate to them. They always invite us to stretch our understanding (sometimes a lot). But they have to be close enough to where our understanding is now for them to be meaningful. John de Ruiter explained that an experience or a dream is like a messenger...bringing a message. My tendency is to focus on the messenger, and perhaps skip over the message. I want to revel in the experience; I want more experiences. But what about the message? The experience seems to feed myself; the message is more about my being. I *could* get quiet inside and explore the message a bit more (it might be subtle); however, I'm busy revelling in the experience with the messenger. Then I'm always looking to meet another messenger.

TIMES PAST

"The Walk" was a cut above all of the churches I had been acquainted with up to that time. One time, John Stevens said (to all of us in "The Walk"), "You've made a big step in coming from the Church Age into The Walk. The step from The Walk into the Kingdom is bigger."

Looking back from NOW I question whether he could see how really BIG the step is. If he did, he wasn't able to convey it to us, or at least not to me. Maybe it wasn't time. Maybe the veils had not yet been lifted enough. Is returning HOME, or being HOME, and living from HOME, initiating the "Kingdom"? In my evaluation......yes. But dare I use that word? Dare I even THINK that word? Dare I think of what's opening up as the Kingdom? I see that it is, but I don't think it's wisdom to use that word. I've heard so much teaching, and so many ideas expressed, about "The Kingdom" that using that word puts a spin on my thinking. It blocks openness to newness. It puts shackles on my mind. Stevens talked of a greater step yet to be taken; we were unable to see it because the veils had not yet been lifted enough. Stevens could not describe the nature of that step--- the veils still clouded it. But we knew what we loved; we knew what we were worshipping; we knew why we worshipped. We were doing what we knew at the time...though veils still obscured the future.

A change is coming. How big it is, and how fast it comes, we can't see yet.

About ten years after John Robert Stevens died, a former "Walk" pastor was meeting with John de Ruiter, and he asked about John Stevens. John de Ruiter went to find John Stevens where he is being. He found John Stevens in some small level of remorse because, although he had a lot of God, and he did a lot, after death he realized that he could have done so much more, if he hadn't made his life so much about himself; if he hadn't relished being known as "The Apostle." Identifying as "myself" and making my life all about me and my life experiences is blinding. Walking with John Robert Stevens was, for me, excellent preparation for meeting John de Ruiter. It seems apparent that John de Ruiter is ushering in something new.

Back in 2005 when I looked in the mirror...into God's eyes (or the eyes of real me), I tried to deny it. Why? It had not been as though I had been seeing me as *the God*, related to my old learned concept of God as an individual separate entity. The seeing did not carry that idea or concept. But rather a seeing, a realization that I am *of God*...made of the same stuff. A little speck of the same; a God-baby; a tiny, tiny bit of MEANING. But why did I try to deny it? Because I want to avoid the responsibility? Or I don't want to go to P.H.D. (Post HOME Development) school? Or was it just that I wanted to cling to my identity as myself, as I've created it? Dr. Eben Alexander (in his book Proof of Heaven) saw much joy and happiness in the next (what he thought of as Heaven). But I can see that I can enter that now, while I'm still living in these dense forms (body, emotions, feelings, will, brain, intuition). I can see that I can enter with some P.H.D. Am I called? I know that I belong. I can see that I belong to something vast beyond imagination. What is the level of my response? I sense a calling to explore more. That's my great opportunity, having been given a little time to be in this realm (Earth). My greatest probability of crossing the threshold will be realized by being in the presence of one who is *being* that, one who has crossed. Being in proximity of one, John, who lives from beyond the threshold. Who easily goes back and forth. Whose home is HOME. Truth. Reality.

I fell asleep in my chair in the middle of the day and I had a dream…a nightmare. I was trying to drive a car but the oppression was on me so heavy, I could hardly manage to control the car. It felt as if every cell in my body was filled with lead and I couldn't move. I *had* to get the car out of traffic. I managed to get it parked on a side walk, and the owner of the business came out and railed on me for parking in front of his door. I woke up and I was still filled with lead so that I could scarcely move. I concluded that it was a direct assault by an entity from another realm. I laid me down at

John's feet and the oppression slowly dissipated …
completely. This kind of thing had happened before. It
happened way back before I met John, when I was walking
with that apostle John Robert Stevens. In those cases I
submitted myself to Jesus, and it slowly dissipated; because
Jesus said "now the prince of this world comes, and he has
nothing in me" (Ref. 6) so I could hide in him. Jesus had no
attitudes, judgments, quirks of behaviour, prejudices, hang-
ups, etc. that the prince of this world could latch onto and
exploit. (Me? Perhaps that's another story; let's not talk
about it). At the present time, I could still submit myself to
Jesus to get clear. But John is here now, and they are being of
the same. They are individuals but they are being oneness.
So why not lay me down at John's feet?

John explained that when we go to sleep we drop our
manufactured identities as 'selves' and revert back to what
we really are. I guess we "remember God's world" as Dr.
Mary Neil expressed it (Ref. 9). I awoke one morning and
myself was not here. Ralph was not here. I was wide awake,
clear and everything was fine. I swung my feet onto the
floor and sat up: I had no relating to myself; no relating to
Ralph. But everything seemed normal and fine. I didn't feel
lost. I clearly did not identify as myself, Ralph. It took a
long, long time --- I would guess 20 to 30 seconds (but how
do you estimate time during profound moments?) to find

myself again and get my orientation back into myself. It was kind of like finding a shirt and putting it on and then being identified by my shirt. Then what I present for the world to see is my shirt. I look in the mirror and gradually come to believe my shirt. I forget real me. Then I spend years making up an intricate story about my shirt. That wouldn't really be necessary; I am me without my shirt. Inside I really *knew* --- I'm real me without my shirt. Looking back, that glimpse was astounding. Looking back later at that experience, I found it amazing; that I could feel so good and so right about *not* identifying as myself. But it took only 20 to 30 seconds to get comfortably back into my illusionary identity as "myself"; to put "Ralph" back on. I can choose to be real minute by minute or hour by hour or, all the time, or only occasionally. However, I handle it inside, I *know.* The easiest way is to give me to John de Ruiter, because he is being That. And, deep inside we already really are all together as One (God-babies) anyway.

I remember that John once asked me, "Do you know who you are?". I responded, "I know who you are and that's enough". He said, "that's *not* enough! You have to know who *you* are!". So, I can see what I am, *that* I am…in beingness the same as he's being. I'm just a little baby in it; he's all grown up.

I've read several books about near-death experiences (N.D.E) over the years. I've concluded that those people just opened their awareness to a deeper level of what we are.

Recently, I had that little dream…that I drowned in a swimming pool and died. Some of my friends and relatives were mourning my death. I was watching the whole thing from above. I was quite okay about all of it: I just didn't have presence and activity in this physical realm, in this the most shallow level of our existence anymore. I could see that I'm real without a body. But then I couldn't talk to my friends anymore. (Perhaps I could if they could hear; but if they were still locked into their identities as "sludge-bunnies", they couldn't let themselves hear.)

Quoting from John de Ruiter's second book "The Intelligence of Love" (Ref.18): "We humans have such an awesome capacity… we have a full spectrum of consciousness. Through the vehicles of the mind, body, emotion, will and intuition, we can experience endlessly expansive or endlessly intricate dimensions of inward and outward movement of being. Within that, as we can later come to know, we have the capacity to share in profound depths of oneness with the universe." ……." the very Truth we are in love with most, has always shown us how to be. What we are REALLY in love with most, is the intimacy of inner rest, softness and tenderness. We are TRULY in love with the only way of being that satisfies and nurtures us completely."

The big step, the step that John Stevens referred to, the step that John de Ruiter calls returning HOME, is a shift of identity. Instead of identifying as myself based on my experiences in this physical life, I shift my identity to Real me. I, as awareness, have myself, but I am not first myself. I am me, awareness, that has a self to live in. I surrender. I cannot see how I could have EVER found the threshold, nor the possibility of crossing it, without being with John de Ruiter. Are there others who can lead thus???? The point is, for me, I found one. My great and awesome good fortune, and to my everlasting delight, is that I met a man, John de Ruiter, who lives from there, and can lead me, guide me into more. Much more. My natural tendency is to quickly match the person I'm meeting; to match what we're being in our hearts. Sometimes, when John walks into a room, I get tuned into him and feel how he's being: So soft, so gentle of heart, so okay, so inviting, loving. It melts me. I cry. A man, taught by Jesus, one with Jesus, commissioned by Jesus to bring (and bringing) a people into…what's NEXT. In proximity to him I sense Profound Joy, so I prefer to be near at every opportunity.

I see that the veils are being lifted and we each have opportunity to identify as the tiny pieces of MEANING that we actually are inside. We can partake of the greatest opportunity which has become available in the history of this planet. And we have one who is able to shine light on our paths: John de Ruiter. A change is coming; how fast and how big, we can't see yet.

Matthew, Mark, Luke and John, authors of the first four Books of the New Testament of the Bible, had revelations and realizations of One (Jesus; leading forth a new step), who was being and manifesting MEANING (as He said we all have opportunity to be and do), so they wrote about it.

I have revelation and realization of one (John de Ruiter; leading forth the next step) who is being and manifesting MEANING here in this physical realm, now, and inviting us to be and do the same, so I thought I should write about it. But I see that there is a great gap between knowing it, understanding it…and *being* it. There is a lot of surrender and letting go between them. I can *like* letting go. I can *like* seeing across the gap.

I've never believed in reincarnation. I remembered that John once commented that if, after death, one could see and realize that he had not returned Home and hadn't engaged in any Post Home Development, that he would give anything, do anything, accept any kind of body or living conditions, live in the most heinous of circumstances and atrocious treatment from others - anything just for another chance to have life in a body in this realm. I've never really believed in reincarnation; however, I've never really rejected it either. It never seemed important. I figured that if I've had multiple life-times and I've used them to perfect my techniques of covering the Truth, of blinding myself, of maintaining my separation from Home, and I've always died having spent none of my time in Post Home Development, what are the chances that in my present life-time I'd reverse all my mini-decisions, abandon my self-training, surrender my living in this tiny part of me that is visible and let my identity open up into the much larger picture of my life, and return Home? The chances are not good. How severely am I, awareness, insisting on being identified as Ralph? As the "self" I've created for me? As a shirt? I *know* that when I lose the body…I lose the shirt, that identity. So whatever level of insistence I hang onto is just silly!

Recently I had a couple dreams regarding the idea of reincarnation. The first was a very brief, small dream and in it I could see and understand that I had been here before, and that I had almost made it into the clean identification of me being and living as only my being. In that life-time I had, however, hung onto some little habits that confirmed my identity as myself; that kept my worldview locked in as "myself". Now, in this life, I could see that I was still hanging onto some little habits and issues and ways of thinking and quirks of behavior which continually confirmed my identification as myself, separate. It looked like it would be touch-and-go whether I would fully surrender this time, to what I actually *know* deep inside.

In the second dream I was a volunteer with a small group who cared for severely crippled people. I arrived at my destination, a concrete, three-room pavilion in a park. I was assigned as a volunteer at this fund-raising breakfast. I was supposed to fry pancakes for anyone who wanted them. I didn't want to be there; I didn't want to fry pancakes; I didn't want to serve breakfast to anyone. I thought that I should find a place where I could smoke a cigarette. In my dream I walked into the next room, a bare room with a concrete floor that hadn't been swept. There were a couple of very crippled people there on the floor. One had a very large head that looked kind of like a three-kilogram baloney. It had a very small, shrunken body that could not move. It lay on the floor and was able to turn its head to lie on one side or the other. I looked into its eyes and they seemed dull and almost lifeless. It was glum and not okay. The other had a very round head, like a balloon, or like a drawing of a kid in a Peanuts cartoon. The head was about three times as large as all the rest of the body, and the body looked like rag doll and was completely useless. This was the most severe cripple I had ever seen or imagined. This person (he or she) could sit if someone propped it up in a corner, but it was out in the middle of this dirty floor, and it kept falling over. It would somehow raise itself up on its rag-doll body and then fall on its face on this dirty floor. I watched it do this several times. I heard it trying to speak but the noises it made were gibberish. And then it would fall down on its face on this dirty floor. I got tuned in on this person, this being, in my dream. It (he or she) couldn't communicate on this physical level; in deeper levels it was communicating volumes. It was being okayness; it was soft and open of heart; it was thankful; it was so very *very* glad, so happy to have been given another opportunity to have life in a body in this realm---even if the body was completely useless. It had joy beyond joy. In my dream something of compassion welled up in me; not a feeling of sympathy, as if I wanted to help this useless person. Something much deeper. Compassion at a completely different level. Understanding. I woke up crying, weeping profusely. This person had more deep understanding than I had. It was REALLY being in okayness, although in physical life it could do nothing. I cried more trying to write the dream down. "The best two days of your life: The day you were born, and the day you found out why." I think this dream helped me see a little more clearly my second-best day.

I did not conclude that these two dreams pointed to confirmation that reincarnation is a valid concept. I did see and realize the truly awesome opportunity I have, living in a body, to give all of me and myself to being the Truth, to allow Meaning to manifest in me. To like; to cherish; to love the opportunity. To give me and myself to the opportunity. So, I stay as close to John de Ruiter as I can. And John made a little suggestion that we could advance our comprehension, our understanding, our being-ness, our souls, in Truth, in one life-time what might take 10,000 years when we have no body; when we have no presence in this physical realm; no existence in this the most shallow level of our existence.

So, I stay with John de Ruiter; to cling to him; to flow into him; to give him my tiny space.

Quoting from John's second book, "The Intelligence of Love" (Ref. 18): "The world is the collective self of all the people in it and, like our selves, is not the purpose for its own existence. The world does not need to change, just as the experience of our selves needs no amelioration. However, as the purpose of the human being awakens, the world responds and changes, just like our selves transform from the influence of our beings.

"There is consciousness in everything. There is knowing in everything, and its purpose is to be given to the deepest meaning it knows. When we give our selves and lives to what we know in our hearts, we are available for our beings. The planet is available for us; the planet is waiting for our awakening. Its nature is inherently open and soft and true, reminding us how to be"
(Ref. 18).

IT's all One. The Origin, the Source of all Life is One. Whatever name we give it (MEANING, YAW, Life, God, Allah, The Force, Um, Atman) IT's all One. We are all born **OF** that. I am **OF** that. Jesus is **OF** that; John de Ruiter is **OF** that. I'm just a baby in It; John is all grown up.

So, I stay as close to John as I can. And, whatever space I give for him to put that in me, or increase that in me, or **BE** that in me, is worth everything. *I like that.*

With Love,
Ralph

REFERENCES

Ref. 1   Ralph Hagloch: "Project FIRE," Convair Astronautics Company Report, San Diego, 1966

Ref. 2   Forest R. Moulton; "An Introduction to Celestial Mechanics," The Macmillan Co., New York, 1914,1959

Ref. 3   Krafft A. Ehricke: "Space Flight: 1. Environment and Celestial Mechanics," D Van Nostrand Co., 1960

Ref. 4   Kenneth J. Collins: "The Evangelical Movement," Baker Publishing Group, Grand Rapids, 2005

Ref. 5   "The Holy Bible, Revised Standard Version," Zondervan Publishing House, Grand Rapids, Michigan, 1952

Ref. 6   "The Holy Bible, King James Version," Cambridge University Press, London

Ref. 7   "Restoration of Original Sacred Name Bible," by Missionary Dispensary Bible Research, 4th Ed., Winfield, Alabama, 1976

Ref. 8   Eknath Easwaran, "The Bhagavad Gita", Nilgiri Press, By the Blue Mountain Centre of Meditation, 2007

Ref. 9   Mary C. Neal: "To Heaven and Back," Waterbrook Press, Colorado Springs,2011

Ref. 10 Huston Smith: "The Illustrated World's Religions," Harper Collins, New York, 1994

Ref. 11 Eben Alexander, M.D. "The Map of Heaven". Simon & Schuster, New York, 2014

Ref. 12 John de Ruiter: "Unveiling Reality," Oasis Publishing, Edmonton, Canada,1999

Ref. 13 "The Quran", Farida Khanam, Editor, Goodword Books, New Delhi, 2012

Ref. 14 Stephen J. Pyne: Voyager, Seeking Newer Worlds in the Third Great Age of Discovery," Viking Penguin Group, New York, 2010

Ref.15 Richard Panek: "The 4% Universe; Dark Matter, Dark Energy, and the Race to Discover the Rest of Reality," Houghton Mifflin Harcourt, Boston, New York, 2011

Ref. 16 Eben Alexander: "Proof of Heaven," Simon & Schuster, New York, 2012

Ref. 17 George A. Hazelrigg, Ph.D. and Ralph S. Hagloch: "Medium Thrust Propulsion Sizing and Performance," Convair Astronautics Company Report, San Diego, 1969

Ref. 18 John de Ruiter. "The Intelligence of Love," Mobius Books, 2015